Taste of Christmas

Cookie

• COOKBOOK •

& Inspiration for the Season

Compiled by Elece Hollis in association with Snapdragon Group℠, Tulsa, OK

Print ISBN 978-1-61626-833-6

eBook Editions:
Adobe Digital Edition (.epub) 978-1-62029-078-1
Kindle and MobiPocket Edition (.prc) 978-1-62029-079-8

Published by Barbour Publishing, Inc., P.O. Box 719, Uhrichsville, Ohio 44683, www.barbourbooks.com

Our mission is to publish and distribute inspirational products offering exceptional value and biblical encouragement to the masses.

Member of the
Evangelical Christian
Publishers Association

Printed in the United States of America.

Taste of Christmas

Cookie
•COOKBOOK•

& Inspiration for the Season

BARBOUR
PUBLISHING

Christmas cookies
and happy hearts,
This is how the holiday starts!

Contents

Fruitcake? Forget about it! Cookies have earned their place in Christmas festivities, and they are here to stay. And why not? They are suitable for sharing around the tree, with neighbors, as the most versatile of gifts, at office parties, and on long trips to Grandma's house, to name just a few of their many uses.

The cookie recipes gathered here are holiday favorites, borrowed from family, friends, coworkers, neighbors, and acquaintances from around the country. Some have been passed down for generations. We hope a few will be a welcome addition to your holiday baking traditions.

Drop Cookies

When they were come into the house, they saw the young child with Mary his mother, and fell down, and worshipped him: and when they had opened their treasures, they presented unto him gifts; gold, and frankincense and myrrh.

Matthew 2:11

Christmas Gumdrop Cookies

2 cups flour
1 teaspoon baking
   powder
1 teaspoon baking soda
1 teaspoon salt
1 cup margarine
1 cup sugar
1 cup packed brown sugar

2 eggs
2 tablespoons water
2 teaspoons vanilla
2 cups quick oats
1 cup red and green
   gumdrops
¼ cup flaked coconut

Mix first four ingredients and set aside. In large bowl cream margarine and sugars until fluffy. Add eggs, water, and vanilla. Blend in dry mixture. Add oats and fold in gumdrops. Shape into 1-inch balls and roll in coconut. Place on greased cookie sheet and flatten with fingertips. Bake at 350 degrees for 10 minutes.

Yield: 4 dozen cookies

Pecan Brittle Cookies

1 cup shortening
1 cup sugar
1 cup packed brown
  sugar
2 eggs
2 cups flour
1 teaspoon baking
  powder

1 teaspoon baking soda
1 teaspoon salt
1 cup cornflakes,
  crushed
1 cup chopped pecans
1 teaspoon vanilla
  extract

Cream shortening and sugars. Add eggs one at a time, beating well after each addition. Stir together flour, baking powder, soda, and salt. Stir cornflakes into flour, coating well. Add dry mixture to creamed mixture. Stir in vanilla. Drop by rounded teaspoons on greased and floured cookie sheet. Bake at 325 degrees for 10 to 12 minutes. Cool on wire rack.

Yield: 10 dozen cookies

Swap Party Oatmeal Macaroons

1 cup shortening
1 cup sugar
1 cup packed brown sugar
2 eggs
1 teaspoon vanilla
2 cups flour
1½ teaspoons salt
2½ cups quick oats

VARIATIONS:
1 cup chocolate chips
½ cup chopped peanuts
1½ cups raisins
¾ cup flaked coconut
1 cup peanut butter chips and
    ½ cup chopped peanuts
1 cup caramel baking chips and ½
    cup chopped pecans

Cream shortening and sugars. Add eggs and vanilla. Sift dry ingredients together and stir in oats. Choose one variation and add those ingredients to batter. Or divide dough into equal parts and choose two or three variations, reducing ingredient amounts proportionately. Drop by teaspoons on greased cookie sheet. Bake at 350 degrees for 12 to 15 minutes.

Yield: 6 dozen cookies

Fruit and Rum Cookies

2 cups chopped pecans
   or walnuts
1 cup golden raisins
¼ cup chopped dates
1 (4 ounce) package chopped
   candied cherries
1 (4 ounce) package chopped
   candied pineapple
½ cup butter, softened

1 cup packed brown sugar
2 eggs
1 teaspoon baking soda
1 teaspoon buttermilk
2 cups flour
1 teaspoon cinnamon
½ teaspoon nutmeg
½ teaspoon allspice
1 teaspoon rum extract

Combine nuts and fruits in bowl. Set aside. Cream butter and sugar. Add eggs. Stir soda into buttermilk. Sift dry ingredients together and add to creamed mixture alternately with buttermilk and rum extract. Drop by teaspoons 2 inches apart on greased cookie sheet. Bake at 325 degrees for 12 minutes.

Yield: 9 dozen cookies

13

Frosted Ginger Drops

½ cup shortening
¾ cup sugar
1 egg
1 cup unsulphured molasses
4½ cups flour
2 teaspoon baking soda
2 teaspoons ginger
1 teaspoon nutmeg

1 teaspoon cloves
1 cup boiling water

ICING:
2 cups powdered sugar
1 tablespoon butter, softened
3 tablespoons milk
1 teaspoon lemon extract

Cream shortening, sugar, egg, and molasses. Add flour, soda, and spices. Stir and add boiling water. Drop by heaping tablespoons on greased cookie sheet. Bake at 400 degrees for 6 to 8 minutes or until browned. To make icing, mix powdered sugar and butter; stir in milk and lemon extract. Let cookies cool before icing.

Yield: 6 dozen cookies

Chocolate Oatmeal Cookies

1¼ cups flour
½ teaspoon baking powder
½ teaspoon salt
⅓ cup cocoa
1¼ cups sugar
1 egg, beaten

½ cup milk
1½ teaspoons vanilla
⅓ cup shortening, melted
⅓ cup butter, melted
2 cups rolled oats

Sift together flour, baking powder, salt, cocoa, and sugar. Set aside. In separate bowl combine egg, milk, and vanilla. Add melted shortening and butter. Add dry mixture. Stir in oats and drop by teaspoons on greased cookie sheet. Bake at 350 degrees for 15 to 18 minutes.

Yield: 5 dozen cookies

Cherry Christmas Cookies

1 cup shortening
2 cups packed brown sugar
2 eggs
½ cup buttermilk
3 cups flour

1 teaspoon baking soda
1 teaspoon salt
1½ cups chopped pecans
2 cups candied cherries
2 cups chopped dates

Cream shortening and sugar. Add eggs and blend well. Add buttermilk. Sift dry ingredients together and gradually add to creamed mixture. Blend until smooth. Stir in pecans, cherries, and dates. Drop by teaspoons on greased cookie sheet. Bake at 375 degrees for 10 minutes or until browned.

Yield: 5 dozen cookies

Holiday Pecan Macaroons

2 egg whites
¾ cup sugar
⅓ cup flaked coconut

½ teaspoon vanilla
20 sweet saltine crackers, crushed
1 cup pecan pieces

Beat egg whites until stiff. Fold in sugar, coconut, and vanilla. Fold in cracker crumbs and pecan pieces. Drop by teaspoons on lightly greased cookie sheet. Bake at 300 degrees for 5 minutes. Cool completely before removing from pan.

Yield: 2 dozen cookies

Fruitcake Cookies

1½ cups packed brown sugar
1 cup butter or margarine
4 eggs, beaten
3 cups flour, divided
3 teaspoons baking soda
1 teaspoon salt
1 teaspoon cinnamon
1½ teaspoons nutmeg
3 tablespoon milk

1 cup golden raisins
1 cup Columbian or regular raisins,
   chopped
1 cup chopped candied cherries
1 cup chopped candied pineapple
1 cup chopped dates
3 cups chopped pecans
⅓ cup orange juice

Cream sugar and butter. Add eggs and blend until smooth. Sift 2 cups flour
with soda, salt, and spices. Add to creamed mixture. Mix fruits and nuts
together and sprinkle remaining 1 cup flour over fruit. Add fruit mixture
to dough along with orange juice. Mix well.
Drop by teaspoons onto greased cookie sheet.
Bake at 325 degrees for 12 to 15 minutes.

Yield: 8 dozen cookies

Christmas Tea Party Cakes

1 cup unsalted butter	1 teaspoon nutmeg
2 cups sugar	1 teaspoon vanilla
4 eggs	4 cups flour
1 tablespoon milk	3 tablespoons baking powder

Cream butter and sugar. Add eggs and blend well. Add milk, nutmeg, and vanilla. Sift flour and baking powder and add to creamed mixture. Drop by teaspoons onto ungreased cookie sheet. Bake at 325 degrees for 15 minutes.

Yield: 4 dozen tea cakes

Frosted Ginger Cookies

½ cup shortening
¾ cup sugar
1 egg
1½ cups molasses
4½ cups flour
2 teaspoons baking soda
2 teaspoons ginger
1 teaspoon cinnamon
1 teaspoon nutmeg

1 teaspoon cloves
1 cup boiling water

ICING:
1 tablespoon butter, softened
2 cups powdered sugar
3 tablespoons milk
1 teaspoon lemon extract

Cream shortening and sugar. Add egg and blend well. Add molasses. In separate bowl mix flour, soda, and spices. Add dry mixture to creamed mixture and stir in boiling water. Drop by teaspoons onto greased cookie sheet. Bake at 400 degrees for 8 to 10 minutes. To make icing, cut butter into powdered sugar; stir in milk and extract.

Yield: 6 dozen cookies

Sugar Cookie Drops

1 cup shortening
2 cups sugar
2 eggs
1 teaspoon vanilla
3½ cups flour

2 teaspoons baking powder
1 teaspoon baking soda
⅛ teaspoon salt
1 cup sour milk
Sugar as needed

Cream shortening and sugar. Add eggs and blend well. Add vanilla. In separate bowl combine dry ingredients. Add dry mixture alternately with milk and blend until smooth. Drop by teaspoons on greased cookie sheet and sprinkle with granulated sugar. Bake at 375 degrees for 10 minutes.

Yield: 6 dozen cookies

Christmastime Chocolate Crisps

½ cup sweet creamery butter,
 softened
1 cup packed brown sugar
1 egg
½ teaspoon vanilla
1 cup flour
½ teaspoon baking soda
2 tablespoons cornstarch

¼ teaspoon salt
½ teaspoon cinnamon
½ cup chopped walnuts
½ pound baker's sweet chocolate,
 coarsely chopped
¼ cup powdered sugar (for dusting)
4 teaspoons chocolate sprinkles,
 optional

Cream butter and sugar. Add egg and vanilla. Blend in all dry ingredients.
Add nuts and chopped chocolate. Mix thoroughly. Drop by teaspoons onto
greased cookie sheet. Bake at 375 degrees for 8 minutes. While warm, dust
with powdered sugar and garnish with chocolate sprinkles.

Yield: 1½ dozen cookies

Christmas Carolers

1 cup shortening
1 cup sugar
1 cup packed brown sugar
2 eggs
1½ teaspoons vanilla
2 cups flour
1 teaspoon baking soda
½ teaspoon baking powder
½ teaspoon salt
2 cups flake cereal with nuts
and dates

2 cups old-fashioned oats
1 cup flaked coconut
½ cup dried cherries, chopped
1 tart apple, peeled, cored,
and chopped
½ cup golden raisins
¼ cup chopped walnuts or pecans,
optional

Cream shortening and sugars. Add eggs and vanilla and blend well. Combine dry ingredients and add to creamed mixture. Gradually add cereal, oats, coconut, cherries, apple, raisins, and nuts. Drop by heaping tablespoons on ungreased cookie sheet. Bake at 325 degrees for 10 minutes.

Yield: 6 dozen cookies

White Christmas Spice Cookies

1½ cups shortening
2 cups sugar
½ cup molasses
2 eggs
2 teaspoons baking soda
4 cups flour

1 teaspoon cloves
1 teaspoon ginger
2 teaspoons cinnamon
1 teaspoon salt
Sugar and powdered sugar
(for dusting)

Cream shortening and sugar. Blend in molasses and eggs. Add dry ingredients and mix well. Divide dough in half. Shape into 1-inch balls. Dredge half in granulated sugar and remaining half in powdered sugar. Place on cookie sheet 2 inches apart. Bake at 350 degrees for 8 to 10 minutes.

Yield: 5 dozen cookies

Santa's Special Request Cookies

2 cups margarine
2 cups sugar
2 cups packed brown sugar
4 eggs
2 teaspoons vanilla
¾ teaspoon salt
2 teaspoons baking powder

2 teaspoons baking soda
5 cups blended rolled oats
1 (24 ounce) package semisweet
    chocolate chips
2 cups chopped pecans
1 (7 ounce) chocolate bar, grated

Cream margarine, sugars, eggs, and vanilla. Gradually add dry ingredients
and mix well. Stir in chocolate chips and pecans. Fold in grated chocolate
bar. Shape into balls from shooter marble to golf-ball size as preferred.
Place on ungreased cookie sheet. Bake at 375 degrees for 10 minutes.
Cool completely before removing from pan.

Yield: 8 dozen cookies

Chocolate Marshmallow Delights

1¾ cups flour
½ teaspoon baking soda
½ teaspoon salt
½ cup cocoa
½ cup shortening
1 cup sugar
1 egg
½ cup milk
1 (10 ounce) package large
   marshmallows
1 cup pecan halves

ICING:
2 cups powdered sugar
5 tablespoons cocoa
⅛ teaspoon salt
4 teaspoons cream
3 tablespoons butter, melted
½ teaspoon vanilla

In medium-sized bowl sift together flour, soda, salt, and cocoa. In large bowl cream shortening and sugar. Add egg and blend well. Add dry mixture to creamed mixture alternately with milk. Drop by heaping teaspoons onto greased cookie sheet. Bake at 350 degrees for 8 minutes. Cut each marshmallow in half and place cut side down atop each hot cookie. Return to oven and bake 2 minutes. Cool. To make icing, mix sugar, cocoa, and salt. Add cream, melted butter, and vanilla. Beat by hand until thick and creamy.

Yield: 4 dozen cookies

Peanut Oat Santa Cookies

1 cup shortening
1 cup sugar
1 cup packed brown sugar
2 eggs
2 cups flour
½ teaspoon salt

1 teaspoon baking soda
1 teaspoon baking powder
1 teaspoon vanilla
1 cup flaked coconut
3 cups rolled oats
½ cup whole raw peanuts, chopped

Cream shortening, sugars, and eggs. In separate bowl combine dry ingredients. Stir into creamed mixture. Add vanilla. Stir in coconut, oats, and nuts. Drop by teaspoons onto greased cookie sheet. Bake at 375 degrees for 8 minutes. Cool on wire rack or platter.

Yield: 5 dozen cookies

Pecan Treasures

¾ cup shortening
1½ cups packed brown sugar
2 eggs, beaten
1 tablespoon milk
2½ cups flour
1 teaspoon cinnamon

½ teaspoon nutmeg
½ teaspoon cloves
½ teaspoon baking soda
½ teaspoon salt
½ cup chopped golden raisins
1 cup chopped pecans

Cream shortening and sugar. Beat in eggs. In separate bowl combine all dry ingredients. Stir into creamed mixture. Add raisins and nuts. Drop by heaping teaspoons onto greased cookie sheet. Flatten slightly with spoon. Bake at 350 degrees for 12 minutes. Cool on wire rack.

Yield: 5 dozen cookies

Snow on Lace

1 cup sugar
2 eggs, beaten
3 teaspoons unsalted butter,
    melted
2½ cups old-fashioned oats

2 teaspoons baking powder
½ teaspoon salt
1 teaspoon nutmeg
1 teaspoon vanilla
⅛ cup powdered sugar (for dusting)

Cream sugar and eggs. Add melted butter and mix well. In separate bowl combine oats, baking powder, salt, and nutmeg. Add to creamed mixture. Stir in vanilla. Drop by tablespoons 2 inches apart onto greased cookie sheet. Bake at 350 degrees for 6 minutes. Cool before dusting with powdered sugar.

Yield: 8 dozen cookies

Chocolate Surprises

½ cup shortening
1 cup sugar
1 egg
1 teaspoon vanilla
1¾ cups flour
½ teaspoon baking soda
½ teaspoon salt
½ cup cocoa
½ cup milk
½ cup chopped pecans

18 large marshmallows, halved

ICING:
2 cups powdered sugar
5 tablespoons cocoa
Dash salt
3 tablespoons butter, melted
4 teaspoons light cream
½ teaspoon vanilla
36 pecan halves

Cream shortening and sugar. Add egg and vanilla. Sift together flour, soda, salt, and cocoa. Add dry mixture to creamed mixture alternately with milk and blend until smooth. Add pecans. Drop by teaspoons onto greased cookie sheet. Bake at 350 degrees for 8 minutes. Top each cookie with marshmallow half (cut side down). Bake 2 minutes longer. Cool. To make icing, sift powdered sugar, cocoa, and salt. Add melted butter, cream, and vanilla. Beat until smooth. Spread icing over marshmallow and top with pecan half.

Yield: 3 dozen cookies

Spicy Raisin Drops

3 cups flour
1 teaspoon baking soda
1 teaspoon cinnamon
1 teaspoon cloves
½ cup shortening or margarine
1½ cups sugar

1 cup milk or half-and-half
3 teaspoons white vinegar
4 tablespoons water
1 cup golden raisins
1 cup regular raisins

Sift dry ingredients together and set aside. In large bowl cream shortening and sugar until light and fluffy. Combine milk, water, vinegar and add to creamed mixture alternately with dry mixture. Stir in raisins. Drop by teaspoons onto greased cookie sheet. Bake at 375 degrees for 10 minutes or until lightly browned.

Yield: 4 dozen cookies

Snow-Topped Christmas Cookies

3 cups flour
1 teaspoon baking soda
1 teaspoon cream of tartar
1 cup unsalted butter
1 cup sugar
1 cup packed brown sugar
3 eggs
1 cup sour cream

ICING:
4 cups powdered sugar
1 teaspoon vanilla
4 to 5 tablespoons milk

Sift dry ingredients together and set aside. Cream butter and sugars until light and fluffy. Add eggs one at a time, beating well after each addition. Add dry mixture alternately with sour cream and blend into thick dough. Drop by rounded teaspoons on greased cookie sheet, leaving room for cookies to spread. Bake at 350 degrees for 8 to 10 minutes. Cool. To make icing, mix sugar, vanilla, and 4 tablespoons milk until smooth. Blend in additional milk if needed.

Yield: 5 to 6 dozen cookies

Holiday Fruit Gems

½ cup butter or margarine
1½ cups sugar
3 eggs
1 teaspoon vanilla

3 cups flour
1 teaspoon baking soda
1 pound dates, chopped
½ cup chopped walnuts

Cream butter and sugar. Add eggs and mix well. Add vanilla, flour, and baking soda. Fold in dates and nuts. Drop by teaspoons onto greased cookie sheet. Bake at 350 degrees for 8 to 10 minutes.

Yield: 4 dozen cookies

Spiced Applesauce Cookies

½ cup unsalted butter, softened
1 cup sugar
1 egg, beaten
1 teaspoon baking soda
1 cup applesauce
2 cups flour

½ teaspoon salt
1 teaspoon cinnamon
½ teaspoon nutmeg
1 cup raisins
½ cup chopped pecans

Cream butter in large mixing bowl. Add sugar and mix well. Add egg.

In small bowl stir soda into applesauce. Add to creamed mixture.

Sift dry ingredients together and stir into creamed mixture.

Fold in raisins and pecans. Drop by heaping tablespoons on greased cookie sheet. Bake at 375 degrees for 10 to 12 minutes.

Yield: 5 dozen cookies

Southern Ambrosia Cookies

1 cup butter, softened
1 cup sugar
1 cup packed brown sugar
2 eggs
1½ teaspoons vanilla
2 cups flour
1 teaspoon baking powder
½ teaspoon baking soda
½ teaspoon salt

1½ cups quick oats
1 teaspoon orange zest
1 teaspoon lemon zest
1 cup flaked coconut
1 cup chopped dates
1 cup golden raisins
¼ cup chopped dried pineapple
1 cup coarsely chopped pecans

Cream butter and sugars until light. Add eggs and vanilla. Combine dry ingredients and stir into creamed mixture. Stir in oats, zest, fruits, and pecans. Mix well. Drop by teaspoons onto greased cookie sheet. Bake at 375 degrees for 8 minutes. Remove from pan and cool on wire rack. Cookies improve with two to three days' storage.

Yield: 5 to 6 dozen cookies

Frosted Lemony Pumpkin Cookies

½ cup shortening
1½ cups sugar
2 eggs
1 cup pumpkin,
    cooked and mashed
1 teaspoon vanilla
1 teaspoon lemon juice
1 teaspoon lemon zest
2½ cups flour
1 teaspoon salt
1 teaspoon cinnamon
1 teaspoon nutmeg

1 teaspoon ginger
½ teaspoon allspice
1 cup raisins
½ cup chopped pecans

LEMON FROSTING:
4 tablespoons butter
2¼ cups powdered sugar, divided
3 tablespoons heavy cream
½ teaspoon lemon zest

Cream shortening. Gradually add sugar. Beat well. Add eggs and beat well. Stir in pumpkin, vanilla, lemon juice, and zest. Sift together flour, salt, and spices. Gradually add to creamed mixture. Fold in raisins and pecans. Drop by teaspoons 2 inches apart on greased cookie sheet. Bake at 375 degrees for 12 to 14 minutes. Cool. To make icing, cream butter and powdered sugar; add cream and zest and beat until smooth.

Yield: 7 dozen cookies

Monta's Molasses Cookies

1 cup plus 4 tablespoons
   unsalted butter
2 cups sugar
1 cup unsulphured molasses
3 large eggs
1 teaspoon vanilla

3½ cups flour
1 teaspoon baking soda
½ teaspoon salt
½ teaspoon mace or nutmeg
2 cups chopped pecans

Cream butter and sugar. Drizzle in molasses and stir. Add eggs and vanilla, beating well. Combine dry ingredients and stir into creamed mixture 1 cup at a time. Stir in pecans. Drop by teaspoons onto greased cookie sheet. Bake at 350 degrees for approximately 8 minutes.

Yield: 10 dozen cookies

Orange Buttermilk Queens

1 cup shortening
2 cups sugar
2 eggs
4½ cups flour
1 teaspoon baking powder
1 teaspoon baking soda

Dash salt
1 cup buttermilk
Zest of 2 oranges, divided
⅔ cup orange juice, divided
1 (16 ounce) package powdered
   sugar

Cream shortening and sugar. Add eggs one at a time, beating well after each addition. Combine flour, baking powder, soda, and salt. Add to creamed mixture alternately with buttermilk until blended. Stir in half the orange zest and half the orange juice. Drop by teaspoons onto greased cookie sheet. Bake at 375 degrees for 10 minutes. To make icing, blend remaining ⅓ cup orange juice and zest with powdered sugar.

Yield: about 8 dozen cookies

Bar Cookies

Thou shalt have joy and gladness;
and many shall rejoice at his birth.

Luke 1:14

Golden Apple Bars

⅔ cup shortening
2 cups packed brown sugar
2 eggs, beaten
1 teaspoon vanilla
2 cups flour
2 teaspoons baking powder
¼ teaspoon salt
1 teaspoon apple pie spice
1 cup chopped green sour apple
   (or yellow apple)
½ cup chopped pecans

Cream shortening, sugar, eggs, and vanilla until fluffy. Sift together flour, baking powder, salt, and apple pie spice. Add to creamed mixture. Fold in apples and pecans. Spread in greased 9x13-inch baking dish. Bake at 350 degrees for 30 minutes. Cool.

Yield: 24 bars

Coconut Honey Bars

1 stick butter	½ teaspoon baking powder
½ cup sugar	½ teaspoon baking soda
1 egg	½ teaspoon salt
½ cup honey	1 cup rolled oats
1 teaspoon vanilla	1 cup flaked coconut
1 cup flour	½ cup chopped pecans or walnuts

Cream butter and sugar. Add egg, honey, and vanilla. Beat until light and smooth. Sift dry ingredients together and add to creamed mixture. Mix well. Fold in oats, coconut, and nuts. Pour into greased and floured 8-inch square pan or, for thinner bars, into greased and floured 9x13-inch pan. Bake for 25 to 30 minutes at 325 degrees or until brown. Serve with whipped topping or ice cream.

Yield: 12 to 24 bars

7 Layer Bars

1 stick butter
1 cup graham cracker crumbs
1 cup milk chocolate chips
1 cup butterscotch chips

1 cup semisweet chocolate chips
1 cup shredded coconut
1 cup pecans (chopped)
1 can sweetened condensed milk

Melt butter in 8x8-inch baking pan. Stir in graham cracker crumbs and pat evenly in bottom. Sprinkle other ingredients (except milk) over crumbs in layers. Pour milk evenly over top. Bake at 350 degrees for 25 to 30 minutes. Let cool and cut into bars.

Yield: 16 bars

First Snowfall Lemon Squares

2¼ cups flour
½ cup sifted powdered sugar
1 cup butter or margarine
4 eggs
2 cups sugar
6 tablespoons lemon juice

2 tablespoons flour
½ teaspoon baking powder
1 tablespoon lemon zest
¼ cup powdered sugar (for dusting)

Combine 2 cups flour and powdered sugar. Cut in butter. Press into 9x13-inch baking pan. Bake at 350 degrees for 25 minutes or until golden brown. With electric mixer beat eggs, sugar, lemon juice, ¼ cup flour, baking powder, and zest at high speed until smooth and buttery looking. Pour over warm crust. Bake at 350 degrees for 25 minutes. Cool before dusting with powdered sugar, using sifter for even snowfall.

Yield: 30 squares

Decadent Holiday Date Delights

1¼ cups flour
⅓ cup sugar
½ cup butter

FILLING:
¼ cup sugar
½ cup packed brown sugar
2 eggs
1 teaspoon vanilla

2 tablespoons flour
1 teaspoon baking powder
½ teaspoon salt
¼ teaspoon nutmeg
1 cup finely chopped dates
1 cup chopped walnuts
2 tablespoons powdered sugar
(for dusting)

Mix first three ingredients until crumbly. Press into greased 9-inch square pan. Bake at 350 degrees for 20 minutes. Cool slightly. To make filling, cream sugars, eggs, and vanilla. Combine flour, baking powder, salt, and nutmeg. Add to creamed mixture. Fold in dates and nuts. Spread as evenly as possible over crust and bake at 350 degrees for 20 minutes longer. Cool and dust with powdered sugar.

Yield: 16 bars

Butterscotch Bars

⅔ cup butter or margarine
1 cup Grape-Nuts cereal
1½ cups light brown sugar
2 eggs
1 teaspoon vanilla

1½ cups flour
1 teaspoon baking powder
¼ teaspoon baking soda
1½ teaspoons salt
1½ cups shredded coconut

Melt butter in saucepan. Add cereal and cook for 2 minutes until cereal is warm and soft. Remove from heat. Stir in sugar and allow to cool. Add eggs and vanilla. Sift together flour, baking powder, soda, and salt. Stir into cereal mixture. Fold in coconut. Spread in greased 9x13-inch baking pan. Press batter into place. Bake at 350 degrees for 25 minutes or until middle is browned.

Yield: 20 bars

Holiday Shortbread Bars

1 cup flour
¼ cup packed dark brown sugar
½ cup unsalted butter
2 eggs
1 cup packed dark brown sugar
2 tablespoons flour
1 teaspoon baking powder

½ teaspoon salt
1 teaspoon vanilla
1 teaspoon orange zest
¾ cup golden raisins
¾ cup regular raisins
½ cup chopped walnuts or pecans
¼ cup sifted powdered sugar

To make crust, combine first two ingredients. Cut in butter until mixture is crumbly. Press into ungreased 9x13-inch baking pan. Bake at 375 degrees for 8 to 10 minutes. Cool slightly. Leave oven on at 375 degrees. Beat eggs until foamy. Add brown sugar, 2 tablespoons flour, baking powder, salt, vanilla, and zest. Beat until thick and lemony colored. Stir in raisins and nuts. Spread over shortbread crust. Return to oven and bake for 20 minutes. While still warm, cut into bars and dust with powdered sugar.

Yield: 30 bars

Fruity Meringue Bars

⅔ cup shortening
⅓ cup sugar
2 eggs, separated
1½ cups flour
½ cup sugar

⅛ teaspoon cream of tartar
1 cup chopped pecans
1 (10 ounce) jar raspberry jam
    (or strawberry, cherry,
    or other berry)

Cream shortening and ⅓ cup sugar until light and fluffy. Add egg yolks and beat well. Mix in flour. Press into ungreased 9x13-inch baking pan. Bake at 350 degrees for 15 minutes or until browned. Beat egg white until frothy with electric mixer at high speed. Gradually add ½ cup sugar and cream of tartar and beat until stiff, glossy peaks form. Fold pecans into egg whites. Spread jam over crust and spread meringue on top of jam. Bake for 25 minutes or until meringue is golden and dry.

Yield: 32 bars

Christmas Cheesecake Bars

⅔ cup packed brown sugar
2 cups flour
10 tablespoons margarine or butter
½ cup coarsely broken pecans
2 (8 ounce) packages cream cheese

1 cup sugar
2 eggs
4 tablespoons lemon juice
1 teaspoon vanilla

Mix first four ingredients until crumbly. Measure out 1½ cups of mixture and set aside for topping. Press mixture into greased 9x13-inch baking pan. Bake at 350 degrees for 12 to 15 minutes. Remove from oven and reduce heat to 325 degrees. Blend cream cheese, sugar, eggs, lemon juice, and vanilla; pour over baked crust. Sprinkle reserved crumb mixture over filling. Bake at 325 degrees for 25 to 30 minutes longer or until center is set.

Yield: 20 to 24 squares

Figgy Pudding Bars

½ cup sugar
2 cups chopped figs
1½ cups water
1 cup butter
2 cups brown sugar
¼ cup milk

1 teaspoon vanilla
2 eggs
1 teaspoon cream of tartar
5 cups flour
2 tablespoons packed sugar

Mix sugar, figs, and water in saucepan. Bring to a boil, stirring to prevent scorching. Cool. Cream butter, brown sugar, milk, vanilla, and eggs. Combine cream of tartar with flour and add to creamed mixture. Divide dough into two parts. Roll out one part and place on greased cookie sheet. Spoon figs over dough and top with second half of rolled-out dough. Sprinkle top crust with 2 tablespoons sugar and bake at 350 degrees for 30 minutes. Cut into squares while warm.

49

Yield: 40 bars

Fudge Pecan Brownies

2 eggs
1 cup sugar
½ teaspoon salt
1 teaspoon vanilla

⅓ cup butter or margarine, melted
¾ cup flour
¼ cup cocoa
1 cup broken pecans

Beat eggs slightly. Add sugar, salt, vanilla, and melted butter.
Stir in flour, cocoa, and pecan pieces. Spread into greased and
floured 9-inch square pan. Bake at 350 degrees for 30 to 35 minutes.
Cool before cutting into 3-inch squares.

Yield: 12 squares

Spicy Nut Triangles

1 cup margarine	2 cups flour
1 cup sugar	1 teaspoon cinnamon
1 egg (separated)	1 cup finely chopped walnuts

Cream together margarine and sugar. Add egg yolk and beat well. Add flour and cinnamon. Spread evenly in jelly roll pan (15x10-inch). Beat egg white slightly and brush over batter with fingertips. Sprinkle nuts over batter and gently press them in. Bake in a slow oven (275 degrees) for about an hour. While still warm, cut into 4 lengthwise strips and 6 crosswise strips. Then cut each piece in half diagonally. These freeze well.

Yield: 48 triangles

Fancy Lemon Bars

2¼ cups flour, divided
½ cup powdered sugar
1 cup unsalted butter
4 eggs
2 cups sugar

⅓ cup lemon juice
½ teaspoon baking powder
2 tablespoons powdered sugar
   (for dusting)

Combine 2 cups flour and ½ cup powdered sugar. Add butter and mix well. Press into greased 9x13-inch baking pan and bake at 350 degrees for 20 minutes. Meanwhile, beat eggs. Add sugar and lemon juice. Mix together ½ cup flour and baking powder. Stir into egg mixture and pour over baked crust. Bake at 350 degrees for 25 minutes or until egg mixture is set. Dust with powdered sugar.

Yield: 32 bars

Chocolate Pizza Squares

1 cup flour
1 cup sugar
⅛ teaspoon salt
⅔ cup shortening
2 eggs
1 teaspoon vanilla

2 (1 ounce) squares unsweetened
    chocolate, melted
½ cup chopped pecans or walnuts
4 cups miniature marshmallows
1 (6 ounce) package semisweet
    chocolate chips, melted

Combine dry ingredients in large mixing bowl. Add shortening and eggs and beat until fluffy. Add vanilla and melted chocolate. Add nuts. Spread in lightly greased 7x11-inch baking pan. Bake at 350 degrees for 20 to 25 minutes. Top with marshmallows. Cool in pan. Drizzle melted chocolate chips over top.

Yield: 32 squares

Toffee Bars

2 sticks butter
1 cup packed dark brown sugar
1 egg
1 teaspoon vanilla

2 cups flour
6 ounces chocolate chips
½ cup chopped pecans

Cream butter and sugar. Add egg and vanilla. Mix well. Add flour and blend well. Spread ¼-inch thick in jelly roll pan, leaving about ½ inch of space around the edges. Bake at 350 degrees for 15 minutes. Immediately after removing from oven, sprinkle chocolate chips evenly over the top. Let stand for 2 minutes and then gently spread melted chocolate around. Sprinkle nuts all over and let cool. Cut into small bars.

Yield: 2 to 3 dozen

Holiday Peppermint Brownies

⅓ cup shortening
1 cup sugar
½ teaspoon vanilla
2 eggs
2 (1 ounce) squares unsweetened
   chocolate, melted
⅔ cup flour
¼ teaspoon salt
⅓ cup walnuts
¼ cup raisins

FILLING:
1 tablespoon cream
1 tablespoon milk, hot
1 teaspoon butter
¼ teaspoon peppermint extract
1 cup powdered sugar

Cream shortening, sugar, and vanilla. Add eggs and beat well. Blend in melted chocolate, flour, salt, nuts, and raisins. Spread into two 8-inch square baking pans lined with wax paper. Bake at 350 degrees for 20 minutes. Each will bake into thin layer. To make filling, cream together all filling ingredients. When layers have cooled, peel off wax paper, add filling, and put layers together.

Yield: 16 bars

Festive Chocolate Macadamia Bars

2⅓ cups flour
⅔ cup sifted powdered sugar
½ teaspoon salt
¾ cup (1½ sticks) cold unsalted
   butter, cubed

Topping:
1 cup plus 2 tablespoons
   sugar
1 cup cream

4 tablespoons butter, melted
1 tablespoon lemon juice
1½ teaspoons vanilla
½ teaspoon salt
3 cups flaked coconut
2½ cups macadamia nut halves,
   toasted
8 ounces white chocolate,
   cut into small (¼-inch) chunks

Grease 9x13-inch baking pan and line with foil. Butter top surface of foil. Combine flour, powdered sugar, and salt. Cut in butter cubes and mix until crumbly. Press into ban. Bake at 350 degrees for 25 minutes. To make topping, combine sugar, cream, melted butter, lemon juice, vanilla, and salt. Add coconut, nuts, and chocolate chunks. Stir until all ingredients are coated. Pour over hot crust and spread evenly. Bake at 325 degrees for 40 to 50 minutes. Cool. Chill for several hours.

Yield: 30 bars

Pecan Turtle Bars

2 cups flour
1 cup packed brown sugar
½ cup butter, softened
1 cup pecan halves

TOPPING:
⅔ cup butter
½ cup packed brown sugar
1 cup semisweet chocolate chips

Beat flour, sugar, and butter at medium speed with electric mixer for several minutes. Press into bottom of ungreased 9x13-inch baking pan. Arrange pecan halves evenly across crust. To make topping, stir butter and brown sugar in saucepan. Bring to a boil for 1 minute, stirring constantly. Pour topping over pecan layer. Bake at 350 degrees for 18 to 20 minutes. Sprinkle chocolate chips on top and allow to stand for 2 minutes or until chocolate begins to melt. Use knife to spread chocolate over surface, leaving some unmelted pieces whole.

Yield: 40 bars

Fancy Chocolate Chip Bars

½ cup shortening
1 cup sugar
1 egg
2 eggs, separated
1½ cups flour
1 teaspoon baking powder

¼ teaspoon salt
1 cup chopped pecans
½ cup semisweet chocolate chips
1 cup miniature marshmallows
¾ cup packed brown sugar

Cream shortening and sugar until fluffy. Add one whole egg and two egg yolks. Beat well. Sift together flour, baking powder, and salt. Add dry mixture to creamed mixture. Spread into greased 9x13-inch baking pan. Mix pecans, chocolate chips, and marshmallows and sprinkle over batter. Whip egg whites at high speed with electric mixer until stiff. Fold in brown sugar. Spread meringue over nut layer. Bake at 350 degrees for 30 to 40 minutes.

Yield: 24 bars

Holiday Cherry Bars

1¼ cups flour
⅓ cup packed brown sugar
½ cup butter
2 eggs
1¼ cups packed brown sugar
1 tablespoon flour
½ teaspoon baking powder
⅛ teaspoon salt
1 cup flaked coconut

½ cup chopped canned cherries
½ cup chopped walnuts

ICING:
2 cups powdered sugar
4 tablespoons butter or margarine
1 teaspoon almond extract
2 tablespoons milk

Combine first three ingredients and press into 9-inch square pan.
Bake at 350 degrees for 15 minutes. Meanwhile, beat eggs and add
1¼ cups brown sugar, 1 tablespoon flour, baking powder, salt, coconut,
cherries, and nuts. Spread over crust. Bake for another 25 minutes
or until browned. To make icing, mix powdered sugar with butter
and almond extract. Add milk and beat until smooth.

Yield: 16 bars

Raspberry Bars

1 cup flour
1 teaspoon baking powder
½ cup butter, melted and cooled
1 egg, beaten
1 teaspoon milk
½ cup raspberry jam

¼ cup butter, softened
1 cup sugar
1 egg, beaten
1 teaspoon vanilla
2½ cups flaked coconut
2 tablespoons powdered sugar

Combine flour and baking powder; gradually stir in melted butter. Stir in egg and milk. Press into bottom of 9x13-inch baking pan. Spread jam on top. Cream butter and sugar. Stir in egg and vanilla. Add coconut and stir well. Spread over jam. Bake at 350 degrees for 30 minutes. Sift powdered sugar over top.

Yield: 2 dozen bars

Orange Slice Cookie Bars

½ cup butter, melted
2 cups packed brown sugar
4 eggs, beaten
2 cups flour

1 pound candy orange slices,
   finely chopped
1 cup chopped pecans
1 cup powdered sugar, sifted

Cream butter and sugar in large mixing bowl. Add eggs one at a time, beating well after each addition. Add flour, chopped orange slices, and pecans. Blend well. Spread evenly in greased 10x10-inch jelly roll pan. Bake at 350 degrees for 25 minutes. Cool. Cut into 2-inch squares. Cut each square in half diagonally to form triangle shapes. Roll in powdered sugar.

Yield: 6 dozen bars

Christmas Orange Pecan Bars

½ cup unsalted butter, softened
¼ cup sugar
1 egg
3 tablespoons orange zest, divided
2¼ cups plus 2 tablespoons
    flour, divided
1½ cups packed brown sugar

2 eggs, beaten
2 tablespoons orange juice
½ teaspoon baking powder
⅔ cup flaked coconut
⅔ cup chopped pecans
2 tablespoons sifted powdered sugar

Cream butter and gradually add sugar, egg, and 1 tablespoon orange zest. Stir in 1½ cups flour. Spread evenly in greased 9-inch square pan. Bake at 350 degrees for 20 minutes. Combine brown sugar and 2 eggs and beat well. Add 2 tablespoons orange zest and orange juice. Stir. Mix in remaining flour and baking powder. Fold in coconut and pecans. Spread over baked crust. Bake at 350 degrees for another 20 minutes.
Cool slightly and dust with powdered sugar.

Yield: 16 squares

Holiday Date Bars

½ cup butter or margarine, melted
1 cup sugar
2 eggs, beaten
1 cup flour

1 teaspoon baking powder
½ teaspoon salt
2 cups chopped dates
½ cup chopped pecans or walnuts

Cream butter and sugar. Add eggs and stir until smooth. Combine flour, baking powder, and salt. Add to creamed mixture. Stir in dates and nuts. Spoon into two greased 9-inch square pans. Bake at 325 degrees for 30 minutes. Cool slightly and cut into 2-inch squares.

Yield: 3 dozen bars

Grandma's Graham Cracker Bars

¼ cup margarine or butter
1 cup graham cracker crumbs
2½ cups flaked coconut
1 (6 ounce) package semisweet
  chocolate chips

1 (6 ounce) package
  butterscotch chips
1 cup chopped pecans
1 (14 ounce) can sweetened
  condensed milk

Melt better in 9x13-inch baking pan. Sprinkle cracker crumbs over butter.
Layer next four ingredients over cracker crumbs. Spoon condensed milk
over all. Bake at 350 degrees for 30 minutes.

Yield: 3 dozen bars

Christmas Apple and Nut Bars

⅔ cup shortening
2 cups packed brown sugar
2 eggs, beaten
1 teaspoon vanilla
2 cups flour

2 teaspoons baking powder
¼ teaspoon salt
1 cup chopped apple
½ cup walnuts

Cream first four ingredients. Sift dry ingredients and add to creamed mixture. Stir in chopped apple and nuts. Spread in greased 9x13-inch baking pan. Bake at 350 degrees for 30 minutes.

Yield: 20 bars

Holiday Apricot Bars

½ cup shortening
1 cup packed brown sugar
2 eggs
1 teaspoon vanilla
1¾ cups flour

2 teaspoons baking powder
½ teaspoon salt
1 cup dried apricots, chopped
½ cup pecans, broken

Cream shortening and sugar until smooth. Add eggs one at a time, mixing well after each. Stir in vanilla. Combine flour, baking powder, and salt. Add to creamed mixture. Fold in nuts and pecans. Press into greased 13x9-inch baking pan. Bake at 350 degrees for 20 minutes.

Yield: 4½ dozen bars

Frosted Coffee Bars

½ cup raisins
Boiling water
1½ cups flour
½ teaspoon baking soda
½ teaspoon baking powder
½ teaspoon salt
½ teaspoon cinnamon
¼ cup shortening
1 cup packed brown sugar
1 egg

1 teaspoon vanilla
½ cup hot coffee
½ cup chopped walnuts

GLAZE:
1 cup powdered sugar
1 tablespoon butter, softened
2 tablespoons milk
½ teaspoon vanilla

Put raisins in mixing bowl with enough boiling water to cover. When raisins cool, drain water off. Sift together flour, soda, baking powder, salt, and cinnamon. Set aside. Cream shortening and sugar until light and fluffy. Add egg and vanilla. Beat well. Add dry mixture alternately with hot coffee. Stir in nuts and raisins. Pour into 9x13-inch baking pan. Bake at 350 degrees for 20 minutes. To make glaze, combine sugar, butter, milk, and vanilla; beat until smooth. Drizzle glaze over cooled bars.

Yield: 32 bars

Layered Cup-a-Candy Cake

½ cup butter
1 cup graham cracker crumbs
1 cup flaked coconut
1 cup chopped pecans

1 cup semisweet chocolate chips
1 (14 ounce) can sweetened
     condensed milk

Melt butter in 9-inch square pan. Sprinkle cracker crumbs evenly over butter. Add coconut, pecans, and chocolate chips in that order. Pour milk over top, coating nuts and chips. Bake at 350 degrees for 30 minutes.

Yield: 30 squares

No-Bake Cookies

*All they that heard it wondered at those things which
were told them by the shepherds. But Mary kept all
these things, and pondered them in her heart.*

LUKE 2:18–19

Coconut Snowballs

2 eggs
¾ cup sugar
1½ cups chopped dates

2 cups crispy rice cereal
1 teaspoon vanilla
½ cup shredded coconut

Combine eggs, sugar, and dates in skillet and mix well. Cook slowly for 10 minutes. Remove from heat and add cereal and vanilla. Drop by heaping teaspoons into shallow dish filled with shredded coconut. Shape into balls and place on tray to cool. Chill until firm.

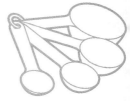

Yield: 2 dozen small cookies

Date Pecan Crisps

1 (8 ounce) package chopped dates
¾ cup sugar
½ cup butter
2 egg yolks, beaten
2 tablespoons milk

2 cups crispy rice cereal
1 cup chopped pecans
2 teaspoons vanilla
1 cup shredded coconut

Combine dates, sugar, butter, egg yolks, and milk in iron skillet. Cook over low heat for 10 minutes, stirring constantly to prevent scorching. Remove from heat and add cereal, pecans, and vanilla. Stir to coat. Cool slightly. Shape into 1-inch balls, roll in coconut, and allow to dry.

Yield: 4 dozen cookies

No-Bake Chocolate Chip Cookies

2 cups sugar
½ cup margarine
½ cup milk
Dash salt
1 cup rolled oats

1 teaspoon vanilla
6 large marshmallows, cut in pieces
1 cup dark chocolate chips
1 cup flaked coconut, optional

In saucepan mix sugar, margarine, milk, and salt. Boil for 3 minutes, stirring constantly to prevent scorching. Remove from heat and add remaining ingredients. Stir until chips are melted and all is coated. Drop by teaspoons on wax paper. Chill to set.

Yield: 3 dozen cookies

Festive Date-Nut Dainties

2 eggs
1 cup sugar
2 cups chopped dates
1 teaspoon vanilla
¼ teaspoon salt

2 tablespoons margarine
2 cups crispy rice cereal
½ cup chopped walnuts
Flaked coconut or vanilla
wafer crumbs

In heavy saucepan beat eggs lightly. Add sugar and dates. Cook for 5
minutes, stirring constantly. Add vanilla, salt, margarine,
cereal, and nuts. Mix well and shape into 1-inch balls.
Roll in flaked coconut or vanilla wafer crumbs.

Yield: 3 dozen cookies

Toffee Surprises

36 saltine crackers
1 cup butter
1 cup packed brown sugar

2 cups semisweet chocolate chips
1 cup chopped pecans

Line cookie sheet with foil and spray with cooking spray. Place crackers in rows on foil-covered pans. Melt butter in microwave, cooking for 2 minutes. Add sugar and stir. Cook for another 2 minutes. Pour syrup over crackers. Bake at 350 degrees for 17 to 20 minutes. Remove from oven and immediately sprinkle chocolate chips over crackers. Top with pecans. Chill for at least 1 hour and break into pieces.

Yield: 36 squares

Macadamia Nut No-Bakes

1 cup sugar
1 cup packed brown sugar
½ cup butter
½ cup soy milk

2 tablespoons carob powder
¼ cup macadamia nut butter
3 cups quick oats

Combine sugars, butter, milk, and carob powder in saucepan. Boil for 2 minutes, stirring occasionally. Remove from heat. Stir in nut butter until smooth. Add oats and stir. Drop by tablespoons on wax paper. Chill.

Yield: 3 dozen cookies

Unbaked Chocolate Slices

½ cup margarine
½ cup sugar
2 tablespoons cocoa
1 egg, beaten
1 teaspoon vanilla

⅔ cup coarsely chopped
 walnuts or pecans
26 graham crackers (13 double
 crackers), coarsely broken

Combine margarine, sugar, cocoa, and egg in saucepan. Beat well. Boil for
1 minute, stirring constantly. Remove from heat and add vanilla, nuts, and
graham cracker pieces. Press into ungreased 9-inch square pan. Chill.

Yield: 26 slices

Christmas Party Cornflake Cookies

½ cup sugar
½ cup light corn syrup
2 tablespoons butter

½ cup crunchy peanut butter
3 cups cornflake cereal

Mix sugar and syrup in saucepan and bring to a boil. Stir in butter and peanut better. Remove from heat. Measure cornflakes into large mixing bowl. Pour sauce over flakes and stir until coated. Drop by tablespoons on wax paper. Chill until set.

Yield: 3 dozen cookies

Caramel Pizzelles

1 (¼ ounce) package active dry yeast
½ cup warm water
1 cup butter
4 cups flour
½ cup sugar
2 eggs

FILLING:
1½ cups packed brown sugar
1 cup butter
1 teaspoon cinnamon
6 tablespoons dark corn syrup

Dissolve yeast in warm water. Cut butter into flour. Blend in sugar, eggs, and yeast mixture. Mix well and let rise for 30 to 60 minutes. Roll dough into balls and bake in pizzelle iron or waffle iron. To make filling, boil brown sugar, butter, cinnamon, and corn syrup until mixture reaches soft ball stage (234 to 240 degrees F). Split waffles in half and spread cut sides with warm filling. Then put halves back together.

Yield: 7 dozen cookies

Chocolate Chippers

1 cup butter
½ cup packed brown sugar
1 teaspoon vanilla

3 cups quick oats
1 cup semisweet chocolate chips
½ cup peanut butter

Melt butter in large saucepan over medium heat. Stir in brown sugar and vanilla. Mix in oats. Cook over low heat for 2 to 3 minutes or until ingredients are blended. Press half of mixture into bottom of buttered 9x13-inch pan. Reserve other half for topping. Meanwhile, melt chocolate chips and peanut butter in small heavy saucepan over low heat, stirring frequently until smooth. Pour chocolate mixture over crust in pan and spread evenly. Crumble remaining oat mixture over chocolate layer, pressing down gently. Cover and chill for 2 hours.

Yield: 32 bars

Raisin-Nut No-Bake Cookies

2½ cups crispy rice cereal
2 cups quick oats
½ cup raisins
½ cup packed brown sugar

½ cup light corn syrup
½ cup crunchy peanut butter
1 teaspoon vanilla

In large bowl stir together cereal, oats, and raisins. Set aside. Combine brown sugar and corn syrup in small saucepan over medium heat. Heat just until boiling; remove from heat. Stir in peanut butter and vanilla until smooth. Pour over cereal and oat mixture; mix well. Press into greased 9x13-inch baking pan using back of large spoon. Cool.

Yield: 30 squares

Chocolate Bourbon Balls

1 (12 ounce) package vanilla
    wafers, crushed
1 cup powdered sugar
2 tablespoons cocoa

1 cup chopped pecans
3 tablespoons light corn syrup
½ cup bourbon
½ cup powdered sugar

Combine wafer crumbs, 1 cup powdered sugar, cocoa, and pecans
in large bowl. Blend well. Combine syrup with bourbon (alcohol
burns out during cooking). Pour over crumb mixture. Mix well.
Shape into 1-inch balls and roll in powdered sugar.

Yield: 4 to 5 dozen balls

Chocolate Chip Mountain Squares

1 (16 ounce) package semisweet
   chocolate chips
1 cup butter
2 cups powdered sugar
2 eggs, beaten

4 cups miniature marshmallows
¾ cup chopped walnuts or pecans
8 double graham crackers
Powdered sugar (for dusting)

Combine chocolate chips, butter, powdered sugar, and beaten eggs in
saucepan. Over low heat stir until chips have melted. Remove from heat
and allow to cool slightly. Add marshmallows and nuts. Line 9x13-inch
pan with graham crackers. Spread chocolate mixture over crackers. Allow to
cool and dust with powdered sugar. Keep refrigerated.

Yield: 24 pieces

Butterscotch Crispies

1 cup sugar
1 cup light corn syrup
½ cup crunchy peanut butter
4 cups crispy rice cereal

1 (16 ounce) package semisweet
  chocolate chips
1 (16 ounce) package butterscotch
  chips

In large saucepan heat sugar and syrup until sugar is dissolved. Stir in
peanut butter and cereal. Spread in ungreased 9x13-inch baking pan.
Melt chips together and spread over top.

Yield: 24 cookies

Chocolate-Dipped Butterballs

1½ cups peanut butter
1 cup butter
1 teaspoon vanilla

6 cups powdered sugar
4 cups semisweet chocolate chips

In large bowl combine peanut butter, butter, vanilla, and powdered sugar. Shape into 1-inch balls and place on cookie sheet lined with wax paper. Stick toothpick into each ball. Place in freezer for at least 30 minutes. Melt chocolate chips in bowl set over simmering water. Stir until chocolate is melted and smooth. Holding toothpick, dip each ball in chocolate, leaving top part undipped. Return to refrigerator until ready to serve.

Yield: 3 to 4 dozen balls

Almond Bark Cookies

1½ pounds almond bark
¾ cup creamy or crunchy
   peanut butter
3 cups crispy rice cereal
2½ cups peanuts

2 cups marshmallows
1 cup dark or semisweet
   chocolate chips
1 teaspoon shortening

Melt almond bark according to package instructions. Stir peanut butter into bark. Mix well and set aside. In large bowl combine cereal, peanuts, and marshmallows. Add peanut butter and bark mixture, coating well. Drop by teaspoons on wax paper. Melt chocolate chips with shortening in microwave on medium heat for 30 seconds. Stir and repeat until melted and smooth. Place in plastic sandwich bag. Snip off one corner to drizzle chocolate over tops of cookies.

Yield: 24 cookies

Hazelnut Holiday Pomanders

1 cup semisweet chocolate chips
½ cup sugar
¼ cup light corn syrup
¼ cup water

1 teaspoon orange extract
2½ cups crushed vanilla wafers
1 cup chopped hazelnuts, toasted
Multicolored decors

Combine chocolate chips, sugar, corn syrup, and water in double boiler and heat until chips are melted. Stir in orange extract and remove from heat. In large bowl mix wafers and hazelnuts. Pour chocolate over wafers and nuts and stir to coat well. Shape into balls and roll in decors to coat.

Yield: 3 dozen cookies

Rocky Road Cookies

20 chocolate sandwich cookies
½ cup chopped pecans, toasted
2¼ cups miniature marshmallows
½ cup butter

4 tablespoons light corn syrup
1 (12 ounce) package semisweet
  chocolate chips

Place cookies in plastic bag and mash with rolling pin. Combine cookie crumbs, pecans, and marshmallows in mixing bowl. In microwavable bowl combine butter, corn syrup, and chocolate chips. Heat for 1 to 2 minutes, stopping to stir chocolate every 20 seconds until smooth. Pour chocolate over crumbs, pecans, and marshmallows. Stir to coat and drop by tablespoons on wax paper. Cool.

Yield: 3 dozen cookies

Peppermint Rounds

1 (14 ounce) can sweetened
    condensed milk
3 cups chocolate wafer cookies,
    crushed and divided
½ cup flaked coconut

½ cup toasted pecans
½ teaspoon peppermint extract
4 cups miniature marshmallows,
    white or colored

Mix all ingredients except 1 cup cookie crumbs. Form into log as thick as
you want your cookies to be. Sprinkle remaining 1 cup cookie crumbs on
sheet of wax paper. Roll log in crumbs. Refrigerate until chilled. Cut into
slices with sharp knife and arrange slices on serving plate.

Yield: 30 cookies

Coconut Chocolate Cookies

2 cups sugar
½ cup cocoa
½ cup butter
½ cup milk

1 teaspoon vanilla
3 cups quick oats
1 cup flaked coconut
½ cup chopped walnuts or pecans

Combine sugar, cocoa, butter, and milk in heavy saucepan.
Boil for 3 minutes. Add vanilla and remove pan from heat.
Mix oats, coconut, and nuts in large mixing bowl. Pour chocolate
mixture over oat mixture. Mix well. Drop by tablespoons on wax paper.

Yield: 4 dozen cookies

Caramel Haystacks

50 graham crackers (25 double crackers)
½ cup coarsely broken pecans
2 tablespoons butter
1½ cups flaked coconut

¼ cup packed brown sugar
2 teaspoons vanilla, divided
½ cup milk
1 cup sugar

Crush graham crackers and combine in large mixing bowl with pecans, butter, and coconut. Combine brown sugar, 1 teaspoon vanilla, milk, and sugar in small saucepan and boil for 1 minute. Add remaining 1 teaspoon vanilla. Pour syrup over crumb mixture and mix well. Shape into small cones and cool on sheet of wax paper. Chill.

Yield: 3 dozen cookies

Bethlehem Haystacks

1 (6 ounce) package
  butterscotch chips
2 teaspoons cooking oil

1 (3 ounce) can chow mein noodles
2 cups miniature marshmallows

Melt chips in double boiler. Stir in oil. In large mixing bowl combine noodles and marshmallows. Drizzle melted butterscotch over noodle mixture and mix thoroughly with fork. Drop by tablespoons on wax paper, reheating over hot water if mixture begins to set up while spooning. Chill haystacks until set.

Yield: 30 cookies

Crispy Christmas Treats

4 tablespoons butter or margarine   ⅓ cup cinnamon imperials
1 (10 ounce) package marshmallows   ½ cup dark chocolate chips
5 cups crispy rice cereal

In heavy skillet, melt butter and marshmallows. Remove from heat
and add crispy rice cereal, stirring to coat. Stir in cinnamon imperials.
Press into buttered 9x13-inch baking pan. Melt chocolate chips in
bowl set over simmering water. Drizzle chocolate over bars and allow
to set before cutting.

Yield: 24 treats

No-Bake Peanut Surprises

1¾ cups sugar
½ cup evaporated milk
4 tablespoons butter or margarine
½ cup crunchy peanut butter

1½ sleeves saltine crackers,
   coarsely broken
1 teaspoon vanilla

In small saucepan combine sugar, milk, and butter and bring to a
boil. Stir in peanut butter. Blend completely. Add crackers and
vanilla. Drop by tablespoons on wax paper. Allow to cool.

Yield: 3 dozen cookies

Fried Cinnamon Cookies

¾ cup sugar
2 eggs
8 egg yolks
3 tablespoons brandy
1 cup whipping cream

5 cups flour
1 teaspoon cardamom or cinnamon
Cooking oil
½ cup powdered sugar

Combine sugar, eggs, egg yolks, and brandy in large mixing bowl. Gradually add cream. Beat well. Combine flour and cinnamon, add to creamed mixture. Chill overnight. Turn out small amount of dough onto floured cloth. Roll out to ¼-inch thickness. Cut into 3-inch diamond shapes. Cut slit in center of each diamond and press one corner through slit. Drop a few at a time into hot oil and fry for 2 minutes. Turn over and allow to brown. Drain on paper towels and dust with powdered sugar.

Serve warm with hot cocoa or coffee.

Yield: 6 dozen cookies

Cream Cheese Treats

2½ cups powdered sugar
1 (3 ounce) package cream cheese,
softened
½ teaspoon vanilla

⅛ teaspoon salt
½ cup shredded coconut
2 dozen pecan halves

Combine sugar, cream cheese, vanilla, and salt. Cover and chill
for 1 hour. Shape into 1-inch balls and roll in coconut.
Press pecan half into top of each cookie.

Yield: 2 dozen treats

Chocolate Peanut Butter Cookies

60 round butter crackers
¾ cup peanut butter
1 (1 pound 4 ounces) package
   white almond bark

Colored sprinkles

Spread 30 crackers with peanut butter and top with second cracker. Melt almond bark in microwave according to package instructions. Dip cookies in almond bark and place on wax paper to cool. Top with sprinkles.

Yield: 30 cookies

Holiday Peanut Treats

1 cup creamy peanut butter
½ teaspoon almond extract
2 tablespoons butter
1¼ cups powdered sugar

2 cups crispy rice cereal
½ cup coarsely chopped
    roasted peanuts

Blend peanut butter, almond extract, and butter in large bowl. Beat in powdered sugar. Stir in cereal, coating well. Line 8-inch square pan with foil. Press dough evenly into pan. Sprinkle with peanuts and press down gently. Chill. Remove foil and loaf from pan. Cut into 1-inch squares.

Yield: 64 treats

Grandma's Chocolate Cornflake Stacks

4 tablespoons butter
¼ cup light corn syrup
4 ounces semisweet chocolate,
    chopped

2¾ cups cornflake cereal

Combine butter, syrup, and chocolate in saucepan. Heat and stir until melted and well blended. Add cereal and stir to coat well. Drop by teaspoons on wax paper. Chill to set.

Yield: 2 dozen cookies

Rolled Cookies

*Through the tender mercy of our God; whereby the dayspring
from on high hath visited us, to give light to them that sit in darkness
and in the shadow of death, to guide our feet into the way of peace.*

LUKE 1:78–79

Simple Cutout Cookies

1 cup butter
1 cup packed brown sugar
2 cups flour
½ teaspoon cinnamon

½ teaspoon ginger
¼ teaspoon cloves
¼ cup cinnamon imperials or raisins

Cream butter and brown sugar. Combine flour and spices and add to creamed mixture. Cover and chill for at least 2 hours. Roll out on floured surface to ¼-inch thickness. Cut into bird and animal shapes. Decorate with cinnamon imperials or raisins. Place on lightly greased cookie sheet and bake at 300 degrees for 12 to 15 minutes.

Yield: 4 dozen cookies

Chocolate Cutout Cookies

1 cup butter
½ cup sugar
½ cup packed brown sugar
1 egg
3 ounces milk chocolate, melted
1 teaspoon vanilla
3¼ cups flour
½ teaspoon baking powder
¼ teaspoon salt

CHOCOLATE FROSTING:
2 tablespoons butter
2 cups powdered sugar
2 tablespoons cocoa
1 teaspoon vanilla
Dash salt
Milk as needed
Colored decors

Cream butter and sugars. Add egg, melted chocolate, and vanilla. Beat well. Combine flour, baking powder, and salt. Add to creamed mixture. Cover and chill for 2 hours. Roll out on floured surface to ¼-inch thickness. Cut into shapes and place 1 inch apart on greased cookie sheet. Bake at 350 degrees for 10 to 12 minutes. Cool. To make icing, cream butter, powdered sugar, cocoa, vanilla, and salt. Add small amounts of milk until icing is proper consistency. Sprinkle iced cookies with decors.

Yield: 3 dozen cookies

Holiday Ginger Thins

½ cup butter
¼ cup shortening
¾ cup packed brown sugar
2 cups molasses
7 cups flour, divided
1 teaspoon salt

2 tablespoons ginger
2 tablespoons cinnamon
1 tablespoon cloves
1 tablespoon baking soda
¼ cup boiling water
½ cup flour (for rolling out dough)

Cream butter and shortening in large mixing bowl. Add sugar and molasses. Beat well. Combine 2 cups flour, salt, and spices. Add baking soda to boiling water and stir to dissolve. Begin adding remaining 5 cups flour to creamed mixture alternately with water-soda solution. Add enough flour to form stiff dough. Divide dough into two parts. Form into logs, wrap in wax paper, and chill overnight. Allow dough to warm for a few minutes.
Roll out on floured surface as thin as possible (about ⅛ inch). Cut into shapes and place 2 inches apart on greased cookie sheet. Bake at 375 degrees for 6 minutes.

Yield: 10 dozen cookies

Pecan Maple Shortbread

5½ cups flour
1 teaspoon salt
1 cup chopped pecans
2 cups butter, softened
1½ cups sugar
½ cup maple syrup

2 egg yolks
½ teaspoon vanilla
2 eggs, lightly beaten
1 cup pecan halves
¼ cup turbinado sugar

Sift flour and salt. Add pecans. In separate bowl beat butter and sugar until light and fluffy. Add syrup, egg yolks, and vanilla. Beat at medium speed until well blended. Gradually add dry ingredients until smooth. Form into two flattened logs. Wrap in wax paper and chill for 2 hours. Slice logs into four parts. Roll out each on floured surface to ¼-inch thickness. Cut into circles with 2-inch biscuit cutter. Place on cookie sheet lined with parchment paper. Brush top of each cookie with beaten egg. Press pecan half into top of each cookie and sprinkle with turbinado sugar. Bake at 350 degrees for 10 to 12 minutes.

Yield: 4 dozen cookies

Anise Seed Almond Cookies

1 cup butter	2 teaspoons salt
1 cup packed brown sugar	½ teaspoon cinnamon
2 tablespoons milk	½ teaspoon nutmeg
2 teaspoons orange zest	½ teaspoon black pepper
2 cups flour	½ teaspoon anise seeds, crushed
1 tablespoon baking powder	½ cup slivered blanched almonds

Cream butter and brown sugar. Add milk and orange zest. Beat well. Combine flour, baking powder, salt, and spices. Gradually add to creamed mixture. Divide dough into two parts and roll out each part on cookie sheet with a lip. Cut into rectangles and press slivered almond into top of each cookie. Heat oven to 425 degrees. Place cookie sheets in oven and reduce temperature to 325 degrees. Bake for 25 minutes. Cool slightly. Break apart.

Yield: 2 dozen cookies

Buttery Pecan Cookies

3 cups flour	2 eggs
1 teaspoon baking soda	1 teaspoon vanilla
¼ teaspoon salt	Colored sugar
1 cup butter	60 pecan halves
2 cups sugar	

Sift dry ingredients and set aside. Cream butter and sugar until fluffy. Add eggs one at a time, beating well after each addition. Blend in vanilla. Stir dry mixture into creamed mixture. Mix well. Form into four logs. Wrap in wax paper and chill for 1 hour. Roll out each log on floured surface to ¼-inch thickness. Cut into shapes and place on ungreased cookie sheet. Sprinkle with sugar and press pecan half into top of each cookie. Bake at 350 degrees for 10 minutes.

Yield: 5 dozen cookies

Grandma's Old-Fashioned Sugar Cookies

6 cups flour
4 teaspoons baking powder
1 teaspoon baking soda
1 teaspoon salt
1 teaspoon nutmeg

1 cup shortening
2 cups sugar
3 eggs
2 teaspoons vanilla
1 cup cream

Sift together flour, baking powder, soda, salt, and nutmeg. Cream shortening and sugar until light and fluffy. Add eggs one at a time, beating well after each addition. Beat in vanilla. Add dry mixture to creamed mixture alternately with cream. Divide dough into four parts. Roll out each part on floured surface to ¼-inch thickness. Cut into circles with 2-inch biscuit cutter. Bake at 400 degrees for 10 minutes.

Yield: 7 dozen cookies

Mocha Fireside Munchies

1 (4 ounce) square sweet baker's chocolate
4 tablespoons butter, divided
1 cup sugar
1 egg

2 tablespoons strong coffee, chilled
2 cups flour
1½ teaspoons baking powder
½ teaspoon cinnamon
4 tablespoons chocolate sprinkles

Combine chocolate with 1 tablespoon butter and melt in double boiler. Set aside. Cream remaining 3 tablespoons butter with sugar. Add egg, coffee, and chocolate mixture. Beat well. In separate bowl combine flour, baking powder, and cinnamon. Gradually add to creamed mixture, blending thoroughly. Chill for 2 hours. Roll out on floured surface to ¼-inch thickness. Cut into shapes and place on lightly greased cookie sheet. Bake at 350 degrees for 12 minutes. Top with chocolate sprinkles while still hot.

Yield: 2 dozen cookies

Grandma's Christmas Ginger Cookies

1 cup unsalted butter
1 cup sugar
2 teaspoons ginger
1 teaspoon cloves

Dash black pepper
1 cup molasses
1 teaspoon baking soda
6 cups flour

Cream butter, sugar, and spices. Measure molasses and stir in baking soda. Stir into creamed mixture. Add flour. Roll out on floured surface and cut into shapes. Place on ungreased cookie sheet. Press raisins into shapes to make eyes, mouths, and shirt buttons. Bake at 400 degrees for 10 minutes.

Yield: 6 dozen cookies

Rolled Ginger Party Cookies

1 cup shortening
1 cup sugar
1 egg
2 tablespoons vinegar
1 cup unsulphured molasses
5 cups flour
1½ teaspoons baking soda
½ teaspoon salt
1 tablespoon ginger

1 teaspoon cinnamon
1 teaspoon cloves

Icing:
⅓ cup butter or margarine
1 cup powdered sugar
Milk as needed
Colored sugars or decors

Cream shortening and sugar until light. Add egg, vinegar, and molasses. Beat well. Sift together flour, soda, salt, and spices. Add to creamed mixture. Mix well and form into several large balls. Chill for 3 hours. Roll out on floured surface and cut into shapes. Place 1 inch apart on greased cookie sheet. Bake at 375 degrees for 5 to 6 minutes. Cool. To make icing, blend butter and powdered sugar. Add small amounts of milk until icing is proper consistency. Decorate iced cookies with colored sugars or decors.

Yield: 8 dozen cookies

Orange Zest Sugar Cookies

1⅓ cups shortening
1⅓ cups sugar
1 teaspoon orange zest
1 teaspoon vanilla
2 eggs
8 teaspoons milk
4 cups flour
3 teaspoons baking powder
½ teaspoon salt

FROSTING:
2 tablespoons butter or margarine
4 cups sifted powdered sugar
1 teaspoon vanilla
Dash salt
¼ teaspoon cream of tartar
1 to 2 teaspoons milk or cream
Food coloring, optional
Colored sugars or decors

Cream shortening, sugar, zest, and vanilla. Beat until light and fluffy. Add eggs and beat well. Combine dry ingredients and blend into creamed mixture. Divide dough into two parts. Chill for at least 1 hour. Take out one part at a time and roll out on floured surface to ⅛-inch thickness. Place on greased cookie sheet. Bake at 400 degrees for 6 to 8 minutes. Cool on wire rack. To make frosting, cut butter into sugar. Add vanilla, salt, and cream of tartar. Beat well. Stir in milk or cream and beat until smooth and soft. Tint with food coloring if desired. Decorate frosted cookies with colored sugars or decors.

Yield: 7 dozen cookies

Midnight Magic Cookies

1 cup butter	2 tablespoons flour
2½ cups light packed brown sugar	4 teaspoons baking soda
6 eggs	9 cups rolled oats
2 teaspoons vanilla	1 cup milk chocolate chips
2 cups crunchy peanut butter	1½ cups chocolate candies

In very large mixing bowl, cream butter and sugar. Add eggs and vanilla, beating well. Add peanut butter and beat again. Stir in dry ingredients, including oats. Fold in chocolate chips. Shape into large balls and press top of each with your palm. Press several candies into top of each cookie. Bake at 350 degrees just until bottoms are lightly browned.

Yield: 10 dozen cookies

Very Berry Shortbread Cookies

1 cup shortening
½ cup sugar
½ cup packed brown sugar
2 egg yolks
3 tablespoons milk
2 teaspoons vanilla
2⅔ cups flour

2 teaspoons cream of tartar
1 teaspoon baking soda
½ teaspoon salt
½ cup raspberry, cherry, strawberry,
    or blackberry jam (or small
    amount of each)

Cream shortening and sugars. Add egg yolks, milk, and vanilla. Combine dry ingredients and add to creamed mixture. Cover and chill for 1 hour. Roll out on floured surface to ⅛-inch thickness and cut into circles with 2-inch biscuit cutter. Cut nickel-sized hole in center of half the cookie rounds. Place ½ teaspoon jam on each whole cookie. Top with second round with hole. Seal edges by pressing with edge of spoon. Place 1 inch apart on greased cookie sheet. Bake at 350 degrees for 10 to 12 minutes.

Yield: 3 dozen double cookies

Christmas Tea Cookies

1 cup butter
2 cups sugar
4 eggs
1 tablespoon milk
1 teaspoon ground nutmeg

1 teaspoon vanilla
4 cups sifted flour
3 tablespoons baking powder
¼ cup pecan halves or maraschino
    cherry halves

Cream butter and sugar. Add eggs one at a time, beating well after each addition. Add milk, nutmeg, and vanilla. Mix well. Combine flour and baking powder and add to creamed mixture. Roll out on floured surface and cut into circles with biscuit cutter. Place on ungreased cookie sheet. Press pecan half or maraschino cherry half into center of each cookie. Bake at 325 degrees for 12 to 15 minutes.

Yield: 4 dozen tea cookies

Cheery Cherry Party Cookies

2 cups dried cherries
2 cups water
3 cups flour
1 tablespoon sugar
½ teaspoon salt
1 cup shortening

½ cup milk
1 (¼ ounce) package active dry yeast
1 egg, lightly beaten
½ teaspoon vanilla
1 cup sifted powdered sugar
(for dredging)

Boil cherries in water until softened. Cool. Combine flour, sugar, and salt. Cut in shortening until crumbly. Scald milk and allow to cool. Add yeast. Stir and let yeast rest for 2 minutes. Add egg and vanilla. Add to flour mixture and mix well. Divide dough into four parts and dust rolling surface with flour or 1 tablespoon powdered sugar. Roll out each part and cut into 10-inch square. Cut each 10-inch square into 2½-inch squares. Put 1 teaspoon cherry filling on each square and fold one corner over filling to opposite corner. Let cookies rest for 10 minutes. Place 2 inches apart on greased cookie sheet. Bake at 350 degrees for 10 to 12 minutes. Dredge in powered sugar while hot.

Yield: 5 dozen cookies

Snow White Christmas Cookies

1½ cups butter, softened
3 cups powdered sugar
4 eggs, beaten
3 cups flour

½ teaspoon salt
3 tablespoons sherry
½ tablespoon nutmeg
Sugar as needed

Cream butter and sugar. Add eggs and beat well. Combine flour and salt.
Add dry ingredients to creamed mixture along with sherry and nutmeg.
Stir just until blended; do not overmix. Chill overnight. Roll out on floured
surface to ⅛-inch thickness. Cut into shapes and place on greased cookie
sheet. Sprinkle with sugar. Bake at 350 degrees for 5 to 8 minutes.

Yield: 80 cookies

Star of Bethlehem Tea Cookies

1 cup butter, softened
1½ cups sugar
3 eggs
3 tablespoons whipping cream

1 teaspoon almond extract
4 cups flour
1 tablespoon baking powder
¼ cup slivered almonds

Cream butter and sugar. Beat until smooth. Add eggs one at a time, beating well after each addition. Add cream and almond extract. Beat well. Sift together flour and baking powder. Add to creamed mixture. Cover and chill for about 4 hours. Roll out on floured surface to ¼-inch thickness. Cut into circles with 2- or 3-inch biscuit cutter. Press five almond slivers in center of each cookie in star pattern. Place on greased cookie sheet and bake at 350 degrees for 10 to 12 minutes.

Yield: 4 dozen cookies

Gingerbread Boys

1¾ cups sugar
¾ cup honey
¼ cup butter
1 tablespoon lemon zest
⅓ cup lemon juice
6 cups flour, divided
3 tablespoons baking powder

⅛ teaspoon salt
2 teaspoons ginger
1 teaspoon cinnamon
½ teaspoon cloves
¼ teaspoon nutmeg
1 egg, beaten
1 egg yolk, beaten

Stir sugar, honey, and butter in heavy saucepan. Bring to a boil, stirring until sugar dissolves. Remove from heat and add lemon zest and lemon juice. Mix well and allow to cool to room temperature. Combine baking powder, salt, and spices. Add egg, egg yolk, and 2 cups flour to creamed mixture. Add remaining 4 cups flour gradually. Form dough into ball and knead lightly on floured surface. Divide into four parts and spread onto cookie sheets lined with parchment paper. Roll out each part to cover whole cookie sheet. Cut out gingerbread boys. Bake at 325 degrees for 20 minutes.

Yield: 6 dozen cookies

Red and Green Sugar Cookies

2 cups flour, divided
1½ teaspoons baking powder
½ teaspoon salt
½ cup butter, softened
1 cup sugar

1 egg
1 teaspoon vanilla
1 tablespoon milk
Red and green food coloring
Sugar as needed

Sift together 1½ cups flour, baking powder, and salt. In separate bowl cream butter, sugar, egg, vanilla, and milk. Add dry mixture to creamed mixture, adding enough of remaining ½ cup flour to make workable dough. Divide dough in half and color each with a few drops of red or green food coloring. Chill for 4 hours. Roll out on floured surface to ⅛-inch thickness. Cut into diamond shapes. Cut each shape in half across center. On greased cookie sheet, place green half with red half. Sprinkle with sugar.
Bake at 375 degrees for 8 to 10 minutes.

Yield: 5 dozen cookies

Meringue Christmas Stars

3 egg whites, room temperature
1 cup sugar
2 teaspoons cinnamon
1 teaspoon lemon zest

1½ cups unblanched almonds,
    ground
2 tablespoons flour
⅛ teaspoon salt

Beat egg whites until soft peaks form. Gradually add sugar, cinnamon, and lemon zest. Remove ½ cup egg whites and set aside. Fold almonds, flour, and salt into remaining meringue. Roll out on floured surface to ¼-inch thickness. Cut with star-shaped cookie cutter. Place stars 2 inches apart on greased cookie sheet. Brush top of each cookie with reserved meringue. Bake at 300 degrees for 20 to 30 minutes.

Yield: 3 dozen cookies

German Pecan Cookies

1½ cups butter
1¼ cups sugar, divided
4 eggs, separated

3 to 3½ cups flour
1½ teaspoons cinnamon
1 cup finely chopped pecans

Cream butter and 1 cup sugar until light. Add egg yolks. Beat until well blended. Add enough flour to make stiff dough. Roll out on floured surface to ¼-inch thickness. Cut into circles with 2½-inch biscuit cutter. Place 2 inches apart on greased cookie sheet. Brush tops with beaten egg white. Combine remaining ¼ cup sugar, cinnamon, and chopped pecans. Sprinkle over tops. Bake at 300 degrees for 15 minutes.

Yield: 5 dozen cookies

White as Snow Christmas Cookies

1½ cups butter, melted
2½ cups sugar
2 eggs
1½ cups whole milk
1 teaspoon vanilla
1 teaspoon lemon juice

5 to 6 cups flour
1 tablespoon baking powder
1 teaspoon baking soda
¼ teaspoon salt
1 egg white, diluted with water
Sugar as needed

Cream butter and sugar. Add eggs and mix well. Pour milk into drinking glass and add vanilla and lemon juice. Sift together 5 cups flour, baking powder, soda, and salt. Add dry mixture to creamed mixture alternately with milk solution. Mix well, adding enough of remaining 1 cup flour to make dough soft and workable. Cover and chill for 2 hours. Roll out on floured surface to ½-inch thickness, adding no more flour than necessary.

Cut into shapes. Brush with egg white diluted with water and sprinkle with sugar. Bake at 350 degrees for 8 to 10 minutes.

Yield: 7 dozen cookies

Walnut Cream Rugelach

2 cups flour
¼ teaspoon salt
1 cup unsalted butter
1 (8 ounce) package cream cheese,
    softened

FILLING:
½ cup sugar
1 tablespoon cinnamon
1 cup chopped walnuts
½ cup chopped raisins

Combine flour and salt. Cut butter and cream cheese into flour mixture.
Mix with fingers until crumbly. Divide crumbly dough into four parts and
flatten into disks. Wrap in wax paper and chill for at least 2 hours. Take out
one disk at a time and roll out on floured surface into 9-inch circle. Use
pizza wheel to cut dough into 12 wedges per disk. To make filling, combine
sugar, cinnamon, walnuts, and raisins. Spread a quarter of filling on top of
each circle. Roll up each wedge, starting with wide end and ending with
point. Place on ungreased cookie sheet and chill for 20 minutes. Then bake
at 350 degrees for 20 to 24 minutes. If desired, dredge cooled cookies in
powdered sugar.

Yield: 4 dozen cookies

Cinnamon Sand Dollars

½ cup butter, softened
1¼ cups sugar, divided
1 egg
1 teaspoon vanilla
2 cups flour

1½ teaspoons baking powder
Pinch salt
1 egg white, diluted with water
1 teaspoon cinnamon

Cream butter and 1 cup sugar. Add egg and vanilla. Blend well.
Combine flour, baking powder, and salt and stir into creamed mixture.
Divide dough into two parts. Chill for 2 hours. Roll out on floured surface
to ⅛-inch thickness. Cut into circles with 2- to 3-inch biscuit cutter.
Place on greased cookie sheet. Brush tops with egg white diluted with
water. Mix remaining ¼ cup sugar and cinnamon. Sprinkle over tops.
Bake at 350 degrees for 10 minutes.

Yield: 3 dozen cookies

Christmas Sugar Cookies

¾ cup shortening
¾ cup sugar
½ teaspoon orange zest
½ teaspoon vanilla
1 egg, lightly beaten
2 tablespoons milk
2 cups flour
1½ teaspoons baking powder
½ teaspoon salt

ICING:
2 tablespoons butter
2 cups powdered sugar
3 tablespoons milk
Colored decors

Cream shortening, sugar, orange zest, and vanilla. Add egg and beat well.
Add milk. Combine flour, baking powder, and salt. Add to creamed mixture.
Stir just until blended. Cover and chill for 1 hour. Roll out on floured
surface to ⅛-inch thickness and cut into shapes. Bake at 375 degrees for
8 to 10 minutes. Cool. To make icing, cut butter into sugar and add milk.
Blend until smooth. Decorate iced cookies with colored decors.

Yield: 2 dozen cookies

Cream Cheese Sugar Cookies

2 cups butter, softened
2 cups sugar
1 (8 ounce) package cream cheese
1 teaspoon salt
1 teaspoon vanilla
1 egg
4½ cups flour

MAPLE FROSTING:
½ cup butter
4 cups powdered sugar
1 teaspoon maple flavoring
2 tablespoons milk
Colored sugars or decors

Cream butter, sugar, cream cheese, salt, vanilla, and egg. Stir in flour and mix well. Divide into two parts and flatten into disks. Wrap in wax paper and chill overnight. Cut one disk in half and return other half to refrigerator. Roll out on floured surface to about ⅛-inch thickness and cut into shapes. Place on ungreased cookie sheet and bake at 350 degrees for 8 to 10 minutes or until golden around edges. Cool. To make frosting, cut butter into powdered sugar. Add maple flavoring and milk. Beat until smooth. Decorate frosted cookies with colored sugars or decors.

Yield: 6 dozen cookies

Chocolate Pinwheels

3 cups flour
2 teaspoons baking powder
½ teaspoon salt
1 cup creamery butter, softened
1 cup sugar

2 eggs, beaten
2 teaspoons vanilla
2 (1 ounce) squares unsweetened
   baker's chocolate, melted
   and cooled

Combine flour, baking powder, and salt. Set aside. Cream butter and sugar until light and fluffy. Add eggs one at a time, beating well after each addition. Stir in vanilla. Gradually add dry mixture to creamed mixture. Divide dough in half. Blend chocolate into one half. Cover and chill for 2 hours. Form dough into two 12-inch logs, one vanilla and one chocolate. Roll out each log on floured surface. Lay chocolate over vanilla. Roll up jelly roll fashion. Wrap in wax paper. Chill for 2 more hours. Slice roll into 24 slices. Place 2 inches apart on greased cookie sheet and bake at 375 degrees for 7 minutes.

Yield: 8 dozen cookies

Festive Caramel Nut Slices

3½ cups flour
1 teaspoon baking powder
½ teaspoon salt
½ cup butter

½ cup shortening
2 cups packed brown sugar
2 eggs
1½ cups chopped walnuts, divided

Combine flour, baking powder, and salt. Set aside. Cream butter, shortening, and brown sugar until fluffy. Add eggs and beat well. Add dry mixture to creamed mixture. Stir in ¾ cup nuts. Divide dough in half and roll each into log about 12 inches long. Spread remaining ¾ cup walnuts on wax paper and roll logs in nuts. Wrap each log in wax paper and chill overnight. Cut each log into 48 ¼-inch slices. Place 2 inches apart on greased cookie sheet and bake at 400 degrees for 4 minutes.

Yield: 8 dozen cookies

Pecan Spice Cookies

½ cup shortening
½ cup sugar
1 cup unsulphured molasses
1 cup sour cream
1 teaspoon cinnamon
¾ teaspoon allspice

¾ teaspoon cloves
1 teaspoon baking soda
Pinch salt
½ cup finely chopped pecans
3½ cups flour

Cream shortening. Gradually add sugar, beating until light and fluffy. Add molasses, sour cream, spices, soda, and salt. Beat well and stir in pecans. Add flour. Divide dough into four parts and chill overnight. Take out one part at a time. Roll out on floured surface to ¼-inch thickness. Cut into star and moon shapes with cutters. Place on greased cookie sheet and bake at 350 degrees for 10 to 12 minutes.

Yield: 7 dozen cookies

Pressed and Shaped Cookies

Unto us a child is born, unto us a son is given:
and the government shall be upon his shoulder:
and his name shall be called Wonderful, Counsellor,
The mighty God, The everlasting Father, The Prince of Peace.

Isaiah 9:6

Walnut Flowers

1 cup unsalted butter
1 cup packed light brown sugar
1 egg
¼ teaspoon salt
2 cups flour

1 cup chopped English or
    black walnuts
1 cup flaked coconut
Sugar as needed

Cream butter and sugar. Beat in egg. Add salt and flour.
Stir in nuts and coconut. Shape into 1-inch balls and crimp
centers and edges with tines of fork dipped in granulated sugar.
Bake at 350 degrees for 15 minutes or until browned.

Yield: 1 dozen cookies

Amish Christmas Cookies

4½ cups flour
1 teaspoon baking soda
1 teaspoon cream of tartar
1 cup butter, softened
1 cup cooking oil
1 cup sugar

1 cup powdered sugar
2 eggs
1 teaspoon vanilla
1 cup chopped walnuts or pecans
½ cup sugar

Combine flour, baking soda, and cream of tartar. Set aside. Cream butter, oil, and sugars until light and fluffy. Add eggs one at a time, beating well after each addition. Stir in vanilla. Gradually add dry mixture. Mix well and stir in nuts. Drop by rounded teaspoons 3 inches apart on greased cookie sheet. Flatten with base of drinking glass dipped in granulated sugar. Bake at 375 degrees for 10 minutes.

Yield: 7 dozen cookies

Snickerdoodles

1 cup shortening
1½ cups sugar
2 eggs
2¾ cups flour
2 teaspoons cream of tartar

1 teaspoon baking soda
½ teaspoon salt
1 teaspoon vanilla
¼ cup granulated sugar
1 tablespoon cinnamon

Cream shortening and sugar. Add eggs one at a time, beating well after each addition. Sift together flour, cream of tartar, baking soda, and salt. Add dry mixture and vanilla to creamed mixture. Stir well. Combine ¼ cup sugar and cinnamon in small bowl. Shape dough into 1-inch balls and roll in cinnamon sugar. Place on ungreased cookie sheet. Bake at 400 degrees for 6 minutes.

Yield: 4 dozen cookies

Pecan Snowballs

1 cup butter
6 tablespoons powdered sugar
2 cups flour
1 tablespoon vanilla

1 cup chopped pecans
Powdered sugar as needed

Cream butter and powdered sugar. Add flour, vanilla, and pecans. Chill for 2 hours. Shape into 1-inch balls and roll in powdered sugar. Place on ungreased cookie sheet. Bake at 275 degrees for 30 minutes and then at 300 degrees for another 10 minutes. Cool. Roll in powdered sugar again.

Yield: 4 dozen cookies

Butter Pecan Fingers

1 cup unsalted butter
¼ cup sugar
Dash salt
1 teaspoon vanilla

1 cup finely chopped pecans
3 cups flour
1 cup powdered sugar, sifted

Cut butter into sugar and salt. Add vanilla and pecans. Add flour. Mix well until crumbly. Shape into fingers about 2½ inches long. Bake at 350 degrees for 15 minutes. Immediately roll each cookie in powdered sugar.

Yield: 2 dozen cookies

French Waffle Christmas Cookies

3 small eggs, separated
3½ cups flour
1 cup sugar
1 cup packed brown sugar

¼ teaspoon baking powder
1 cup butter, melted
1 teaspoon vanilla

Beat egg yolks in small bowl until thick. Set aside. Beat whites until foamy. Set aside. Combine flour, sugars, and baking powder. Stir in melted butter, egg yolks, and vanilla. Fold in egg whites until well blended. Cover and chill for 8 hours. Shape into 1-inch balls. Heat and lightly grease waffle iron. Add several balls at a time, one in each quarter of iron, and cook until browned. Cool and serve with vanilla ice cream.

Yield: 6 dozen cookies

Christmas Eve Pretzel Cookies

1 cup butter
2 cups sugar
4 eggs
4 cups flour
2 teaspoons baking powder

1 teaspoon cinnamon
½ teaspoon cloves
½ teaspoon nutmeg
1 cup ground pecans
Powdered sugar as needed

Cream butter and gradually add sugar. Beat well. Add eggs one at a time, beating well after each addition. Combine flour, baking powder, and spices. Add to creamed mixture. Fold in pecans. Shape into 1-inch balls. Flatten each ball into rope about 10 inches long. Twist into pretzel shape. Place on greased cookie sheet. Bake at 350 degrees for 10 to 12 minutes. Cool and dust with powdered sugar.

Yield: 5 dozen cookies

Apricot Balls

1 (8 ounce) package dried apricots,
   finely diced
2½ cups flaked coconut

¾ cup sweetened condensed milk
1 cup finely chopped nuts
   (pecans work especially well)

Mix together apricots, coconut, and milk.
Shape into 1-inch balls and roll in nuts. Refrigerate.

Yield: 2 dozen.

Cherry Christmas Dainties

1 cup butter or margarine
½ cup sugar
2 eggs, separated
1½ teaspoons vanilla
½ teaspoon salt

2½ cups flour
1 teaspoon baking powder
2 cups finely chopped pecans
40 candied cherries, cut in half

Cream butter and sugar. Add egg yolks, vanilla, and salt. Blend in flour and baking powder. Shape into 1-inch balls. Dip in beaten egg white and roll in pecans. Place on greased cookie sheet and press cherry half into center of each. Bake at 350 degrees for 20 to 25 minutes.

Yield: 6½ dozen cookies

White Chocolate Apricot Treats

¾ cup unsalted butter, softened
½ cup sugar
½ cup packed brown sugar
2 eggs
1 cup flour

1 teaspoon baking soda
2½ cups quick oats
2 cups white chocolate chips
1 cup chopped coarsely
    dried apricots

Cream butter and sugars until fluffy. Add eggs one at a time, beating well after each addition. Stir in flour and soda. Add oats, chips, and dried apricot bits. (You can also use dried apples, cranberries, cherries, or mixed fruits.) Shape into 1-inch balls and place on ungreased cookie sheet. Bake at 375 degrees for 7 to 9 minutes.

Yield: 3 dozen cookies

Grandma Brink's Filled Cookies

½ cup butter
1 cup sugar
1 egg
3½ cups flour
2 teaspoons cream of tartar
1 teaspoon baking soda
⅛ teaspoon salt
½ cup sour milk

1 teaspoon vanilla

FILLING:
2 cups sugar
1 cup chopped raisins
½ cup hot water
1 tablespoon flour

Cream butter and sugar. Add egg and blend well. Combine flour, cream of tartar, soda, and salt. In drinking glass combine milk and vanilla. Add dry mixture to creamed mixture alternately with milk and vanilla. Chill for at least 2 hours. Roll out on floured surface to ¼-inch thickness. Cut into circles with 2-inch biscuit cutter. To make filling, combine sugar, raisins, hot water, and flour in saucepan. Cook until smooth and creamy. Spoon about 1 teaspoon filling on half the rounds and top with second round. Seal edges by pressing with fork tines. Prick top of each cookie with fork. Bake at 375 degrees for 18 to 20 minutes.

Yield: 5 dozen cookies

Santa's Favorite Sugar Cookies

1 cup margarine or butter
1 cup cooking oil
1 cup powdered sugar
1 cup sugar
3 teaspoons vanilla
2 eggs

4 cups flour
1 teaspoon cream of tartar
1 teaspoon baking soda
½ teaspoon salt
Sugar as needed

Cream butter and oil with sugars and vanilla. Add eggs one at a time, beating well after each addition. Combine dry ingredients and add to creamed mixture. Shape into 1-inch balls. Flatten with patterned bottom of drinking glass dipped in granulated sugar. Bake at 350 degrees for 10 minutes. Note: Dough will be too soft to cut with cookie cutters.

Yield: 6 dozen cookies

Holiday Ribbons

½ cup butter, slightly softened
½ cup sugar
1 cup packed brown sugar
2 eggs
1 tablespoon lemon juice
1 teaspoon vanilla

3 cups flour
½ teaspoon baking soda
½ teaspoon cinnamon
½ teaspoon allspice
Red decorating sugar

Cream butter and sugars until smooth. Add eggs one at a time, beating well after each addition. Add lemon juice and vanilla. Sift together flour, soda, and spices. Stir into creamed mixture and load into cookie press. Press onto greased cookie sheet in 12-inch pieces shaped like ribbon candy. Bake at 350 degrees for 8 to 10 minutes or until edges are lightly browned. While warm, cut into 3-inch segments. Sprinkle with red decorating sugar.

Yield: 9 dozen cookies

Santa Winks

2½ cups flour
1 teaspoon baking powder
½ teaspoon baking soda
½ teaspoon salt
¾ cup shortening
1 cup sugar
2 eggs
2 teaspoon milk

1 teaspoon vanilla
1 cup chopped pecans
1 cup chopped dates
¼ cup chopped maraschino cherries
½ cup crushed cornflakes
and ½ cup flaked coconut
¼ cup maraschino cherries,
cut in half

Sift dry ingredients together and set aside. Cream shortening and sugar. Add eggs, milk, and vanilla. Beat well. Add dry mixture and mix thoroughly. Add pecans, dates, and chopped cherries. Place cornflakes in one cereal bowl and coconut in another. Shape dough into balls and drop into flakes or coconut. Place on greased cookie sheet and press cherry half into center of each cookie. Bake at 375 degrees for 12 to 15 minutes.

Yield: 5 dozen cookies

Snowflake Pizzelles

3 eggs
¾ cup sugar
½ cup butter (don't use oil),
   melted and cooled

1 teaspoon vanilla
1 teaspoon anise seed or extract
1¾ cups flour
2 teaspoons baking powder

Cream eggs and sugar. Add cooled melted butter, vanilla, and anise. Sift flour and baking powder and add to creamed mixture. Batter will be stiff enough to be dropped by spoon. Heat and lightly oil waffle iron or pizzelle iron. Cook long enough to brown both sides and turn out to cool on paper towels. Batter can be refrigerated and used at a later time.

CHOCOLATE VARIATION: Omit anise and add 3 tablespoons cocoa and 3 tablespoons granulated sugar. If desired, substitute chocolate flavoring for vanilla extract.

Yield: 30 pizzelles

Candy Cane Cookies

1⅓ cups butter or margarine
1⅓ cups sugar
2 whole eggs
2 egg yolks
1½ teaspoons vanilla

4 cups flour
1 teaspoon baking soda
½ teaspoon salt
Red food coloring

Cream butter and sugar. Add whole eggs, egg yolks, and vanilla and beat well. Combine flour, baking soda, and salt. Blend dry mixture into creamed mixture. Divide dough into two parts and tint one part with red food coloring. Wrap each in wax paper and chill for 2 hours. Shape dough into thin ropes each about 6 inches long. On greased cookie sheet gently twist two ropes (one red and one white) together into candy cane shapes. Bake at 350 degrees for 10 to 12 minutes.

Yield: 6 dozen cookies

Date Pinwheel Cookies

FILLING:
1½ cups chopped dates
¾ cup honey
⅓ cup water
1 teaspoon lemon juice
½ cup finely chopped walnuts

COOKIE BATTER:
1 cup shortening
2 cups packed brown sugar
3 eggs
4 cups flour
1 teaspoon cinnamon
1 teaspoon baking soda
4 tablespoons powdered sugar
(for dusting)

In saucepan cook dates, honey, and water until dates are soft. Remove from heat and add lemon juice and nuts. Set aside. Cream shortening and sugar until fluffy. Add eggs one at a time, beating well after each addition. Combine dry ingredients and add to creamed mixture. Divide dough in half and chill for half an hour. Roll out each half on floured surface to rectangle about 10x12 inches and ½ inch thick. Spread filling over rectangles. Roll up each rectangle jelly roll fashion and wrap in wax paper. Chill overnight. Cut log into thin slices and place on ungreased cookie sheet. Bake at 375 degrees for 12 minutes. Remove from pan to cool and dust with powdered sugar.

Yield: 4 dozen cookies

Angel Wings

1 cup unsalted butter, softened
1 cup packed brown sugar
1 cup sugar
2 eggs
1 teaspoon vanilla

4 cups flour
1 teaspoon baking soda
1 teaspoon cream of tartar
1 teaspoon salt
Sugar as needed

Cream butter and sugars. Add eggs one at a time, beating well after each addition. Add vanilla. Sift dry ingredients together and add to creamed mixture. Mix well. Shape into balls. Dip one side in water and then in sugar. Place 2 inches apart on greased cookie sheet, sugar side up. Use fingertips to press each ball into shape of wings. Bake at 375 degrees for 12 minutes.

Yield: 4 dozen cookies

Pecan Mandelbrot

2½ cups flour
1 tablespoon baking powder
3 eggs
1 cup sugar
2 teaspoons vanilla

½ cup cooking oil
1 cup broken pecans, toasted
½ teaspoon cinnamon
2 teaspoons sugar

Sift flour and baking powder and set aside. Use electric mixer with whipping attachment to beat eggs for about 2 minutes until light yellow. Gradually add sugar. Beat for another 2 minutes. Add vanilla and oil and beat half a minute longer. Reduce mixer speed and gradually add flour mixture. Fold in cooled toasted pecans. Cover and chill for 1 hour. Form dough into three (16-inch) logs and place on greased baking pans. Combine cinnamon and sugar and sprinkle over logs. Bake at 350 degrees for 20 minutes. Cool for 5 minutes. Reduce oven temperature to 325 degrees. Use bread knife to cut logs diagonally into ½-inch thick slices. Lay slices on their sides. Sprinkle cut sides with more cinnamon sugar. Return to oven and bake for 8 to 10 minutes. Turn slices over and bake for another 6 to 8 minutes until crisp.

Yield: 96 cookies

French Macaroons

1 cup blanched almonds
1 cup sugar
2 egg whites, beaten lightly

½ teaspoon vanilla
2 tablespoons powdered sugar

Line a baking sheet with parchment paper. Combine almonds, sugar, egg whites, and vanilla in a food processor and pulse until it has the texture of a very coarse paste. Blend the paste on high speed for 2 minutes, until it is very smooth and thick. Drop by spoonfuls onto baking sheet, forming 1-inch mounds. Allow the batter to rest, uncovered, for 10 minutes. Bake at 400 degrees for 12 minutes. Allow to cool before dusting with powdered sugar.

Yield: 8 servings.

Chocolate Pistachio Biscotti

2½ cups flour
1 teaspoon baking powder
¼ teaspoon baking soda
½ teaspoon salt
¾ cup unsalted butter
2 teaspoons orange zest
2 teaspoons lemon zest

1 cup sugar
2 eggs
1 teaspoon vanilla
1 cup coarsely chopped unsalted
   pistachios, toasted
1 (3½ ounce) square bittersweet
   chocolate, shaved

Sift together flour, baking powder, soda, and salt and set aside. Mix butter with zests until smooth. Gradually add sugar and beat for 1 minute longer. Add eggs one at a time, beating well after each addition. Add vanilla. Add flour mixture in three parts and stir just until blended. Fold in nuts and shaved chocolate. Chill for 1 hour. Divide dough into three parts and form each into 14-inch log. Place on jelly roll pans or cookie sheets lined with parchment paper. Bake at 350 degrees for 25 minutes. Cool slightly. Reduce oven temperature to 300 degrees. Cut logs into ½-inch slices. Place cut sides up on pan and bake for another 15 minutes. Turn slices over and bake for another 7 to 10 minutes.

Yield: 74 slices

Jam Thumbprints

1 (8 ounce) package cream cheese
¾ cup butter, softened
1 cup powdered sugar
2¼ cups flour

½ teaspoon baking soda
½ cup chopped pecans
½ teaspoon vanilla
Jam or preserves

Beat cream cheese, butter, and powdered sugar until smooth. Add flour and baking soda; mix well. Add pecans and vanilla. Chill dough for about 30 minutes. Shape dough into 1-inch balls and place on ungreased cookie sheet. Press thumb in middle of each cookie. Fill with about 1 teaspoon of your favorite jam or fruit preserves. Bake at 350 degrees for 14 to 16 minutes.

Yield: 3 dozen.

Cherry-Crowned Pecan Cookies

1 cup butter, softened
½ cup sugar
½ cup light corn syrup
2 eggs, separated

2½ cups flour
2 cups finely chopped pecans
Candied or maraschino cherries,
   drained

Cream butter and sugar. Add corn syrup and egg yolks. Beat well.
Add flour gradually. Shape into 1-inch balls. Dip in beaten egg whites
and roll in pecans to coat. Place on greased cookie sheet 2 inches apart.
Bake at 325 degrees for 20 to 25 minutes.

Yield: 4 dozen cookies

Butter Pecan Snowed-In Cookies

¾ cup butter
¼ cup sugar
¾ cup ground pecans
2 teaspoons cold water

2 teaspoons vanilla
1¾ cups flour
Dash salt
1 cup powdered sugar

Cream butter. Add sugar and beat until light and fluffy. Stir in pecans, water, and vanilla. Stir in flour and salt. Shape small amounts of dough into 2-inch sticks. Place on ungreased cookie sheet. Bake at 300 degrees for 25 to 30 minutes. Cool and roll in powdered sugar.

Yield: 5 dozen cookies

Cranberry Honey Cookies

½ cup shortening
½ cup butter
1 cup packed light brown sugar
⅓ cup honey
3 eggs
1 teaspoon vanilla
1 teaspoon cinnamon

1 cup dried cranberries
1 cup chopped pecans
1 cup flaked coconut
4 cups flour
1 teaspoon baking soda
1 teaspoon salt
Sugar as needed

Cream shortening, butter, brown sugar, honey, and eggs. Stir in vanilla, cinnamon, cranberries, pecans, and coconut. Combine dry ingredients and add to creamed mixture. Mix well. Chill for 1 hour. Shape into 1-inch balls and roll in granulated sugar. Place on ungreased cookie sheet and bake at 350 degrees for 12 minutes.

Yield: 6 dozen cookies

Pepper-Nut Slices

2 cups sugar
1 cup packed brown sugar
3 eggs
1 teaspoon mace
1 teaspoon nutmeg
1 teaspoon cinnamon
1 teaspoon allspice
1 teaspoon anise
1 cup dark corn syrup

1½ cups butter
1 teaspoon cardamom
1 teaspoon salt
1 teaspoon cloves
1 teaspoon ginger
1½ teaspoons baking powder
1½ teaspoon baking soda
10 cups flour

Combine all ingredients and enough flour to make stiff dough. Knead well until smooth. Let stand overnight in cool place. Form into long rolls about 1 inch wide. Cut into thin slices and bake at 350 degrees for 6 to 8 minutes.

Yield: 8 dozen cookies

Cookie Swap Party Recipe

2 cups butter, softened
1 cup sugar
1 cup packed brown sugar
2 eggs

4 cups flour
½ teaspoon salt
1 teaspoon baking soda

Cream butter and sugars. Add eggs and dry ingredients. Divide dough into six parts. To each add one of following to make six different types of cookies to swap: ½ cup flaked coconut; ½ cup raisins; ½ cup chopped pecans or walnuts; ½ cup chocolate chips; ½ cup butterscotch, white chocolate, or toffee chips; 1 teaspoon ground cinnamon. Form each into log about 1½ inches in diameter. Chill overnight. Cut into slices and bake at 350 degrees for 8 to 10 minutes.

Yield: 1 dozen cookies per roll

Holiday Spritz

1 cup shortening
¾ cup sugar
1 egg
1 teaspoon vanilla
2¼ cups lour

1 teaspoon baking powder
½ teaspoon salt
1 egg yolk, beaten
Colored decorating sugar

Cream shortening and add sugar gradually. Beat until light and fluffy. Add egg and vanilla. Sift together flour, baking powder, and salt. Add to creamed mixture. Stir thoroughly. Load cookie press and press in swirls on ungreased cookie sheet. Brush tops with egg yolk and sprinkle with colored sugar. Bake at 350 degrees for 12 to 15 minutes.

Yield: 7 dozen cookies

Notes

Notes

Notes

Notes

Notes

Notes

Notes

Notes

Recipe Index